"For every heart that's ever longed for more, for every woman who's asked 'Is this all there is?' about her faith, for every one of us who longs for less fear and more courage, Sharon Jaynes's words and wisdom can be the catalyst God uses to take you from just 'okay' to the best He has for you. Get ready to have your world rocked in a way that will make you never want to go back to the way things were before."

Holley Gerth, *Wall Street Journal* bestselling author
of *You're Already Amazing*

"Take Hold of the Faith You Long For is an absolute triumph. It is a declaration of truth and freedom for every battle-worn believer who longs to make it to the Promised Land. Jaynes gently yet firmly leads her readers through the desert and into the land of Canaan, teaching us to march seven times around the walls of today's Jericho and to seize the promises the Lord has for us. A must-read."

Emily T. Wierenga, founder of The Lulu Tree and author
of *Atlas Girl* and *Making It Home*

"What this world needs is more women who courageously believe God is the path to living boldly, bravely, and beautifully. Sharon Jaynes challenges and cheers us to let go of our weaknesses and trade them for God's strengths."

Pam Farrel, author of 40 books, including 7 *Simple Skills for Every Woman: Success in Keeping It All Together*

"If you've ever come to a point in your Christian walk where you've stopped and thought to yourself, 'Is this really it?' you will be so blessed by Sharon's incredible story of how God called her out of the mundane and into the extraordinary. You too will be left challenged and inspired to walk in faith in a whole new way."

Jennifer Rothschild, author of *Lessons I Learned in the Dark*;
Self Talk, Soul Talk; and *Invisible: How You Feel
Is Not Who You Are*; founder of Fresh Grounded Faith
events and womensministry.net

"We have all known what it's like to be stuck and discouraged in our Christian walk while desiring a faith that's intimate with Jesus, enriched with experience, and dynamic with power. In her book *Take Hold of the Faith You Long For*, Sharon Jaynes shows us how to go from a sluggish faith to one that's truly alive. She offers hope, inspiration, and fresh perspective for faith-worn believers."

Heidi St. John, speaker, author, and creator
of *The Busy Mom* blog

"If you are ready to move beyond a stagnant, struggling faith, read this book. Filled with biblical depth, relatable stories, and practical strategies, *Take Hold of the Faith You Long For* is a powerful narrative that will help you shake off lackluster believing and put on the full-and-abundant-life faith that Christ died for you to experience."

Gwen Smith, speaker, worship leader, cofounder of Girlfriends
in God, and author of *I Want It All* and *Broken into Beautiful*

TAKE HOLD

OF THE

FAITH

YOU

LONG

FOR

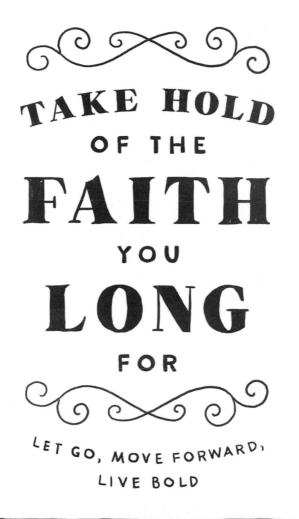

TAKE HOLD
OF THE
FAITH
YOU
LONG
FOR

LET GO, MOVE FORWARD,
LIVE BOLD

SHARON JAYNES

BakerBooks

a division of Baker Publishing Group
Grand Rapids, Michigan

© 2016 by Sharon Jaynes

Published by Baker Books
a division of Baker Publishing Group
P.O. Box 6287, Grand Rapids, MI 49516-6287
www.bakerbooks.com

Printed in the United States of America

Library of Congress Cataloging-in-Publication Data
Names: Jaynes, Sharon, author.
Title: Take hold of the faith you long for : let go, move forward, live bold / Sharon Jaynes.
Description: Grand Rapids : Baker Books, 2016. | Includes bibliographical references.
Identifiers: LCCN 2015050531 | ISBN 9780801018855 (pbk.)
Subjects: LCSH: Christian women—Religious life.
Classification: LCC BV4527 .J396 2016 | DDC 248.8/43—dc23
LC record available at http://lccn.loc.gov/2015050531

Unless otherwise indicated, Scripture quotations are from the Holy Bible, New International Version®. NIV®. Copyright © 1973, 1978, 1984, 2011 by Biblica, Inc.™ Used by permission of Zondervan. All rights reserved worldwide. www.zondervan.com

Scripture quotations labeled AMPC are from the Amplified Bible, Classic Edition (AMPC). Copyright © 1954, 1958, 1962, 1964, 1965, 1987 by The Lockman Foundation.

Scripture quotations labeled ESV are from The Holy Bible, English Standard Version® (ESV®), copyright © 2001 by Crossway, a publishing ministry of Good News Publishers. Used by permission. All rights reserved. ESV Text Edition: 2011

Scripture quotations labeled KJV are from the King James Version of the Bible.

Scripture quotations labeled Message are from The Message by Eugene H. Peterson, copyright © 1993, 1994, 1995, 2000, 2001, 2002. Used by permission of NavPress Publishing Group. All rights reserved.

Scripture quotations labeled NASB are from the New American Standard Bible®, copyright © 1960, 1962, 1963, 1968, 1971, 1972, 1973, 1975, 1977, 1995 by The Lockman Foundation. Used by permission.

Scripture quotations labeled NIV 1984 are from the Holy Bible, New International Version®. NIV®. Copyright © 1973, 1978, 1984 by Biblica, Inc.™ Used by permission of Zondervan. All rights reserved worldwide. www.zondervan.com

Scripture quotations labeled NKJV are from the New King James Version®. Copyright © 1982 by Thomas Nelson, Inc. Used by permission. All rights reserved.

Scripture quotations labeled NLT are from the Holy Bible, New Living Translation, copyright © 1996, 2004, 2007 by Tyndale House Foundation. Used by permission of Tyndale House Publishers, Inc., Carol Stream, Illinois 60188. All rights reserved.

Italics in quoted Scripture reflect the author's emphasis.

In keeping with biblical principles of creation stewardship, Baker Publishing Group advocates the responsible use of our natural resources. As a member of the Green Press Initiative, our company uses recycled paper when possible. The text paper of this book is composed in part of post-consumer waste.

16 17 18 19 20 21 22   7 6 5 4 3 2 1

To my mom,
Louise Anderson Edwards.
In her last days, she reminded me once again,
"It's not how you start; it's how you finish."
She finished well.
1932–2014

Contents

one

Stuck on a Feelin'

I was alone, or at least I felt that way. Women huddled in happy clusters chatting about first one thing and then another. Some propped babies on their hips. Others clutched Bibles in their hands. Most wore smiles on their faces. I wore one too. But it wasn't a reflection of what was in my heart. The upturned lips were simply the camouflage I wore to blend in—to avoid being found out. What I really wanted to do was run and hide. On the outside I was a well-put-together church mom with trendy shoes and snappy jeans, but on the inside I was a little girl cowering in the far recesses of the playground hoping no one would notice my reluctance to join in.

What's wrong with me? I wondered. *Why don't I feel the joy these other women feel? What holds me back from experiencing the confidence and assurance they seem to experience? Why do they seem so happy? Where is that abundant life Jesus talked about? If I am a new creation like the Bible says, why don't I feel like one? Why do I continue to act like the same old me, struggle with the same negative emotions, and wrestle with the same old sins? Why do I feel like I'm wandering around in a maze trying to find a way out of these feelings of inadequacy?*

The problem was, I was stuck. Yes, I had professed Jesus as my Lord and Savior. I had done that. I knew Christ had set me free, but honestly, I couldn't tell you exactly what He had set me free from. He had set me free from the penalty of sin and spending eternity in hell. I got that. But I had a niggling feeling that was not what Jesus meant when He said, "You will know the truth, and the truth will set you free" (John 8:32). I had a hunch He meant something more than heaven when He said, "I have come that they may have life, and have it to the full" (John 10:10). That sounded earthy to me.

My early years in the faith were filled with wonder, expectancy, and downright giddiness. But somewhere along the line, I had settled into being a good church girl—a Bible-study mom who moved into cul-de-sac Christianity, pitched my lawn chair under a shade tree, and waved at other well-mannered believers doing the same. Year after year I hoped, *Maybe this will be the Bible study that will make it all better.* And the truth is, I didn't even know what the "it" was.

What do you do when your walk becomes a crawl? When you feel like you are a disappointment to yourself and to God? When spiritual chronic fatigue leaves you wondering if it's all worth it? When you feel stuck between the Red Sea and the Promised Land—saved from slavery but never quite making it to the land of milk and honey? What do you do when you realize your once-passionate faith has morphed into the safe confines of a predictable, domesticated belief system, far away from "Go ye therefore" and "Greater things than these"?

Sometimes the gap between the faith we long for and the faith we experience seems vast, beyond bridging. We stand on the east ledge of the great expanse, thinking the west rim is out of reach or possibly not worth the effort. We think going from where we are to where we want to be is impossible, implausible, or unrealistic, so we pull up a lounge chair in the land of in-between and settle in.

Content, but not really. Longing, but not quite enough. Satisfied, but not completely. We settle for reading about the adventures of others and secretly wonder if they are on the up-and-up. We read about the bold faith of others and think, *Good for them*. We make peace with passivity because we falsely believe God would never want to use the likes of us anyway.

I'd hazard a guess that most believers don't really want to venture out of the land of in-between. Given the choice, they wouldn't go back to the Egypt of their life before Christ, but at the same time, they don't really want to get their shoes messy and step into the unknown, unabridged faith of Promised Land living. Many settle for a milquetoast faith that listens through the walls to the music from a party going on in the next room. So what if they can't catch all the words? They get the gist of the melody, and they're okay with that. They aren't particularly motivated to move beyond weekend visits with God, as if they're a kid whose parents have shared custody. They're satisfied circling in the wilderness; after all, it's certainly better than Egypt. They're satisfied with a bit of manna and a splash of water every now and then. There *is* heaven to come. Yes, at least there is that. And that's enough.

But I'm not that person. I'm hoping you're not either.

How do we move beyond the safe confines of cul-de-sac Christianity and into the mountain-moving, giant-slaying, lame-man-leaping, adventurous faith? How do we stop circling in the wilderness of unbelief and make our way into the Promised Land of peace, purpose, and a passionate faith? How do we refuse to be lulled into the ridiculous idea that God is a safe, simple, grandfatherly gentleman who kisses babies and helps us find the closest parking space at the mall and matching towels at a clearance sale? How do we consistently access the power of God's promises and boldly believe the truth? How do we stop being held hostage by feelings of inferiority, insecurity, and inadequacy and take hold of the confidence and courage to live bold and do all God has planned for us to do and be all God has created us to be? How do we move beyond *knowing* the truth to actually *believing* it? These are some of the questions we will tackle in the pages ahead, finding answers that turn stumbling blocks into stepping-stones that lead to "life to the full."

We can get stuck in the land of in-between in many ways and for many reasons, and to move beyond them we must be brave enough to let go and take hold. Let go of the lies that hold us hostage and take hold of the truths that set us free. Let go of festering offenses and take hold of forgiving grace. Let go of shame-filled ponderings and take hold of grace-filled pardon. Let go of weighty worry and take hold of total trust. Let go of the preoccupation with self-doubt and take hold of the power-filled promises of God. Let go of comparing ourselves to others and take hold of our uniqueness fashioned by God. Let go of ungrateful grumbling and take hold of unceasing praise. Let go of paralyzing doubt and take hold of fleet-footed faith that's ready to dance to the daring rhythm of God's drum.

Jesus said, "I am the way and the truth and the life" (John 14:6). He wasn't simply speaking of the eternal life we receive when we leave this earth but the fullness and freedom we can experience in the here and now when we take hold of all He has taken hold of for us.

The Greatest Show on Earth

Have you ever watched a circus performer on a flying trapeze? A short horizontal bar suspended by ropes or straps dangles high above the crowd. The aerialist grabs the trapeze bar, jumps off a high platform, and swings through the air. She swings out once, swings back above the platform, and swings out again. The fun begins for those below during the peak of the third swing. The performer releases the bar midair and grabs hold of another bar or the hands of a second performer hanging from his knees who swings toward her.

Once she grabs hold, the crowd remembers to breathe. Somersaults, backflips, and triple twists wow the crowd. And each move requires the performer to let go and grab hold—let go of one bar or pair of hands and grab hold of another. Without the faith to do so, the trapeze artist would simply swing back and forth until the pumping momentum gave way to dangling or hang stuck in between two platforms with hands clinging to both bars. Not the greatest show on earth.

Paul wrote to the Philippians, "I press on to *take hold* of that for which Christ Jesus *took hold* of me" (Phil. 3:12). Another version expresses the verse this way: "I press on to lay hold of (grasp) and make my own, that for which Christ Jesus (the Messiah) has laid hold of me and made me His own" (AMPC). When you take hold, grasp, and make your own all of what Jesus has already taken hold of for you, you begin to experience life to the full—the faith you've always longed for. If we would *grasp and make our own* what Jesus has already done for us, and what He has deposited in us, our lives would look very different from the tepid faith of the average churchgoer.

It's not enough to know the promises of God; you've got to grab hold with all the firmness of the trapeze artist—release what is behind and take hold of what is ahead. *That* is the greatest show on earth. That is how the greatest faith on earth becomes a reality.

God's promises are not automatic. We must move from knowing the promise, to believing the promise, to actually taking hold of the promise through obedient action in order to make it a reality in our lives. God told Joshua about the Promised Land, "I will give you every place where you set your foot" (Josh. 1:3). He and the Israelites had to "set their feet" to conquer the land—to take hold of the promise that was theirs for the taking.

God's power, provision, and purposes are for "whosoever will" (Mark 8:34 KJV). Will what? Will let go of all that holds us back from experiencing the abundant life of the adventurous faith and take hold of the truth that makes it so.

Paul wrote to the Corinthian church, and to you and me, "'What no eye has seen, what no ear has heard, and what no human mind has conceived'—the things God has prepared for those who love him" (1 Cor. 2:9). Another translation says, "What eye has not seen and ear has not heard and has not entered into the heart of man, [all that] God has prepared (made and keeps ready) for those who love Him [who hold Him in affectionate reverence, promptly obeying Him and gratefully recognizing the benefits He has bestowed]" (AMPC).

Every one of those plans God has *prepared, made, and keeps ready* requires us to let go of one thing and take hold of another. It was this truth that gave me the courage and confidence to leave the comfortable land of in-between—to let go of simply being a nice church girl and venture into the purpose God had planned for me all along.

The Truth behind the Pretty Door

Like many children living through the depression in rural North Carolina, my parents graduated from high school and said "I do" at the altar a few weeks later. Ten months passed and they heard their first baby's cry. Five years after my brother was born, I made my grand debut. Of course, I don't remember my arrival, but I understand it was a snowy day in the 1.4-square-mile rural town of Spring Hope, North Carolina.

My family lived in a nice neighborhood, in a ranch-style house with white columns supporting the extended front porch and sixty-foot pine trees forming a shady canopy overhead. Azaleas burst to life each spring and encircled the perimeter of our home with a palette of fuchsia, pink, and white blossoms. With two kids and a collie named Lassie, our family looked like the typical All-American family. While the house was a Southern picture of tranquility, inside the walls brewed an atmosphere of hostility and fear.

From the very beginning my parents had a tumultuous marriage. I don't remember much about my first five years of life, but I do remember many heated arguments, violent outbursts of anger, and periods of passive-aggressive silence. I am sure there were happy times tucked in the marred pages of my childhood, but the accumulation of dark days overshadowed the bright ones and eventually snuffed out their existence in my memory. What I do remember is hiding in my closet, holding my hands over my ears, and squeezing my eyes shut tight in an effort to block the visual images that accompanied the volatile voices.

My father didn't drink every day, but when he did, a temper that perpetually seethed just below the surface erupted into a rage. It seemed that anger constantly smoldered behind his eyes, and alcohol stoked the fire until it would combust with sudden flames of violence. My parents fought both verbally and physically in my presence, and I saw many things a little child should never see and heard words a little child should never hear. I remember going to bed, pulling the covers up tightly under my chin, and praying that I would hurry up and go to sleep to shut out the noise of my parents fighting. On several occasions, I awoke to broken furniture, my mother's black eye, and a weeping father making promises that it would never happen again. It did.

My father was a self-made man who rose from driving a delivery truck at a lumberyard to becoming part owner and manager of a building supply company. He was a tough cookie, and I was afraid of him. And even though I kept my distance, I longed to have a daddy who loved me like the ones I saw walking with their little girls in the park, kissing their little princesses on the cheek when they dropped them off at school in the morning, or snapping their photos at special events.

As a child, I always felt I was in the way. While my physical needs were cared for, my heart ached for more. I wasn't sure what that *more* was, but I did know it was not a fancy dress, a new toy, or a shiny trinket.

I never felt pretty enough, smart enough, or talented enough. When I tried to help around the house, it seemed I never did it quite right. I remember my mom throwing up her arms in desperation and shouting a common declaration of parents throughout the ages: "What's wrong with you?" And in my little-girl mind I thought, *I don't know, but something is.*

The strands of inferiority, insecurity, and inadequacy began to weave an invisible yet indelible grid system over my mind. Every thought I had, every comment by others, every social interaction had to filter through that sieve of deficiency before it was interpreted by my little-girl mind. By the time I was twelve years old, that filter was cemented firmly in place. I was a scared and scarred little girl who kept her mouth shut by day and her eyes squeezed closed by night.

But God didn't leave me that way.

But God

Two of my favorite words in the Bible are *but God*. His intervention begins in Genesis 3:9 and continues through the pages of the Bible, throughout the annals of history, and in our lives today. My "but God" story began when I was twelve years old. I became friends with a cute little redhead in my neighborhood named Wanda Henderson. We had known each other since first grade, but our lifelong friendship truly began in the sixth grade. One thing I loved about Wanda was her family. Her parents loved each other and seemed to really enjoy each other's company. I was drawn to their love like a starving child to bread.

And while I didn't understand why that family was so different from mine, I knew it had something to do with Jesus. Mrs. Henderson flitted about doing her housework while singing little praise songs to God and buzzed about with a joyful hum. She praised God for the smallest details and seemed to be so happy. But one thing that was a bit odd to me was that she talked *to* Jesus and *about* Jesus as though she knew Him personally.

Amazingly, as messed up as my family was with the alcohol, fighting, and a host of other vices that infested our home, we went to church on Sunday . . . looking good. We heard ear-tickling, non-offensive sermons that were moral enough to make us feel we'd done our American duty but not spiritual enough to convict or transform us in any way. We walked through the massive double doors of the pristine sanctuary and were greeted with smiling folks in their Sunday best. "How are you today?" they'd ask. "Fine, just fine," we'd reply. But we were anything but fine, and I suspect the families with spit-shined children sitting in the pews around us weren't either.

I spent as much time as possible at the Hendersons' home. After a Saturday night sleepover, Mrs. Henderson invited me to go to church with their family. It was there that I witnessed a sea of people who seemed to know Jesus personally. She wasn't the only one! When they said they were "fine," they seemed to mean it. Happy people. Joy-filled people. Men and women who still struggled with life but had a deep hope within. And somewhere along the line, it dawned on me. My family had a religion. This family had a relationship with Jesus. And that made all the difference.

I wanted what they had, and I found every excuse possible to tag along with the Hendersons on Sunday mornings. My mind was a thirsty sponge for Scripture and my heart a well-tilled field for seed. For the first time, I caught a glimpse of a *heavenly Father* who

19

loved me—who loved me so much that He gave His one and only Son as a sacrifice for me. I soaked in the truth that Jesus willingly died on Calvary's cross to pay the penalty for my sin so I could live in heaven for all eternity. I marveled at the fact that God loved me, not because I performed well but just because I was His.

I confided in Mrs. Henderson about what was going on in my home. Many nights I ran down to their house when the tension in my home grew volatile or when I was afraid. This woman took me under her wing and shared the love of Jesus with me. It wasn't that she was making a special effort to love me. It was just who she was. I never felt like I was her pet project or that she had a four-point witnessing plan to get me saved. She was just herself—a redheaded, spunky bundle of joy who oozed Jesus's love and left the residue of His glory wherever she went. Honestly, looking back at those tumultuous days, I am not sure I would have wanted my daughter to have a relationship with the likes of me. I was headed for trouble, but Mrs. Henderson, without even being aware of what she was doing, headed Satan off at the pass.

One night, when I was fourteen years old, Mrs. Henderson sat me down on her den sofa and asked, "Sharon, are you ready to accept Jesus as your personal Savior and Lord?"

With tears streaming down my cheeks, I answered, "Yes, I am."

With her guidance, I confessed my sin, acknowledged my need for a Savior, asked Jesus to be my Lord, and received the promise of eternal life. The next day I went home and told my mom what I had done.

At first, my parents were leery of my newfound faith, but my love for the Lord was hard to resist or deny. Three years after I gave my life to Jesus, my mother accepted Jesus as her Savior. Then three years after her decision, through a series of twists and turns that only our heavenly Father could have orchestrated, my earthly father gave his life to Christ. In a matter of six years, God had worked an incredible miracle in my life and my family's life.

Set Free but Not Living Free

What a great story! The sheer wonder of it stokes my passion for Jesus and gratitude to God every time I tell it. But let's go back to that fourteen-year-old girl who was bound with chains of inferiority, insecurity, and inadequacy—the girl who had a filter of worthlessness over her mind and heart. When I made the decision to believe in Jesus Christ as my Lord and Savior, did those feelings dissolve like springtime snow? Oh, dear friend, I wish I could tell you they did, but they did not. As a matter of fact, I didn't even know those chains were there. I simply knew something wasn't quite right. I was held hostage by my self-perceived deficiencies and didn't even know it.

After the initial excitement of making a commitment to Christ settled down a bit, I actually felt a little worse about myself. Now I added a new "I'm not good enough" to the list of my inadequacies. *I'm not a good enough Christian*, I decided. *I can't memorize Scripture like other people or pray like other Christians. I keep struggling with the same old insecurities. I know God loves me, but I don't think He likes me very much. Why should He? I don't like me much either.* The problem was, as the song says, I was stuck on a feelin'. I walked through life prodded by my emotions rather than led by the truth.

Through the years, I learned to compensate for my insecurities and self-perceived inadequacies. If you had seen me as a teenager— my achievements and accomplishments—you never would have known that I felt that way about myself. But even though I had the borders of the puzzle in place with the promise of heaven, I felt like I was missing key pieces to complete the picture. From the time I was fourteen until I was in my early thirties, I always felt like there was something wrong with me spiritually. I had an uneasiness—like I had walked into a movie twenty minutes late and was trying to figure out what was going on. I wondered why I struggled to live the victorious Christian life. By my midthirties, I had a wonderful husband, an amazing son, and a happy home life. I attended Bible studies and even taught a few. But in my heart, I knew something wasn't quite right. I wonder if you've ever felt that way.

Simply put, I was stuck. I was stuck in my spiritual growth, and the harder I spun my wheels, the deeper they sank in the muck and mire of the land of in-between—saved from the slavery of Egypt but never quite making it to the Promised Land. And then God brought another woman into my life to shimmy the plank of truth under my tires and help me get on my way.

God wants to show you truths about *your* true identity, His timeless sufficiency, and your preordained destiny that flesh and blood cannot reveal. He sits by the well waiting for you to show up so He can dip down deep and pour out the affirmations you're thirsting for—affirmations that call you to let go of the hindrances that hold you hostage, to take hold of the promises that set you free, and to live bold with that faith you've always longed for. He's looking for men and women who are not only *willing* but also *hungrily yearning* to step outside of the quiet, settled, predictable faith and into the boldly believing, courageously confident, and miraculously powerful adventurous faith. Who will take hold of what they've already got—of what Jesus has already taken hold of for them.

The Bible tells us, "For everything that was written in the past was written to teach us, so that through the endurance taught in the Scriptures and the encouragement they provide we might have hope" (Rom. 15:4). As we look at the stories of modern-day men and women who have broken free of the confines of the mediocre faith, we are also going to take the hand of several biblical men and women who have done the same.

Throughout the pages of this book, we're going to join Moses fireside and eavesdrop on his conversation with God by the burning bush. Through Moses's objections to his calling, and God's answers to his doubt, we'll discover several important lessons that will work the truth of Scripture under our stuck faith and get us moving forward in an adventurous, thriving, intimate relationship with Christ.

two

Who Do You Think You Are?

Let Go of Your Insecurity and Take Hold of Your True Identity

If ever there was a man who was stuck on a feelin', it was Moses. We find his story in Exodus, the second book of the Bible. Exodus 1:1 begins with the word "Now," which can also be translated "And" (NKJV). Some translations leave out the conjunction, but in the Hebrew, the original language of the Old Testament, that little word is a hand reaching back to join Exodus to Genesis. It is a reminder that Exodus is simply a continuation of God's redemptive story through His chosen people—the Israelites. The narrative picks back up 430 years after the final words of Genesis, and something is afoot.

> Then a new king, who did not know about Joseph, came to power in Egypt. "Look," he said to his people, "the Israelites have become

much too numerous for us. Come, we must deal shrewdly with them or they will become even more numerous and, if war breaks out, will join our enemies, fight against us and leave the country. (Exod. 1:8–10 NIV 1984)

Pharaoh put slave masters over the Hebrews to oppress them with forced labor—making bricks and mortar for large edifices and tending the king's fields. But the harder the Egyptians worked them, the stronger the Hebrews became, the more numerous they grew, and the farther they spread.

Oh, how I would love to camp out on that point, but for now, just remember that what the enemy would like to use to destroy you, God will use to make you stronger.

Pharaoh came up with Plan B. He called for two midwives, Shiphrah and Puah, and commanded, "When you are helping the Hebrew women during childbirth . . . if you see that the baby is a boy, kill him; but if it is a girl, let her live" (Exod. 1:16).

However, the midwives feared God more than they feared Pharaoh and allowed the boys to live. When questioned by the king, they explained that the Hebrew women were vigorous and had their babies before they could get to them. So God was kind to the midwives, and the people grew stronger, spread farther, and multiplied faster. (Gotta love it!)

Foiled again, Pharaoh went to Plan C and gave this order: "Every Hebrew boy that is born you must throw into the Nile, but let every girl live" (v. 22). And all that happened in chapter 1!

In chapter 2, we meet a woman we later learn is named Jochebed. This brave heroine gave birth to a beautiful baby boy. She hid him in their home for three months but knew the day was quickly approaching when she would not be able to keep him stowed away. Pharaoh's edict weighed heavy on her heart, and she came up with a plan. Yes, she would obey Pharaoh's command, but first she would make her babe his own personal little ark. With nimble fingers she wove a basket of papyrus leaves and covered it with tar and pitch. Then she placed the infant into the Nile and prayed that someone . . . anyone . . . would come by and save her baby.

Miriam, the baby's big sister, hid in the bulrushes to watch over her brother. What happened next is Ephesians 3:20 in Technicolor: "Now to him who is able to do immeasurably more than all we ask or imagine, according to the power that is at work within us . . ." Who should come along but the one person in the entire kingdom who could do whatever she wanted—Pharaoh's daughter. When she and her attendants came to the water's edge to take a sponge bath, a baby's cry drifted by.

Spotting the floating basket, the princess ordered her attendant to fetch it from the Nile. When she pulled back the blanket, she saw the beautiful baby boy. "This must be one of the Hebrew babies," she surmised. Right then and there she decided to adopt him as her own.

On cue, the watchful Miriam sprang from behind the bushes. "I know where you can get a wet nurse for the baby," she offered.

Excitedly, Miriam ran back to get her mother and brought her to the princess.

"Nurse this baby for me," she explained, "and I will pay you wages. Bring him back to me when he is weaned. He will become my son."

(Notice, the first five heroes in the book of Exodus are really heroines: the two midwives, Jochebed, Miriam, and Pharaoh's daughter.)

We don't know the baby's name prior to his adoption, but Pharaoh's daughter named him Moses, which means "drawn out of water." Moses grew up as royalty and was "educated in all the wisdom of the Egyptians and was powerful in speech and action" (Acts 7:22).

He Failed and He Bailed

Something happened to Moses when he was forty. He discovered that he was not really an Egyptian but a Hebrew . . . and that changed everything. Moses came up with a plan to save his people. God did not call him to this plan. He came up with it all on his own.

One day Moses was walking among his people and saw an Egyptian beating a Hebrew slave. Glancing first one way and then the other to make sure no one was looking, Moses killed the Egyptian and hid him in the sand. One down. Several million to go. Moses was working the plan.

The next day Moses was out walking among his people and saw two Hebrews fighting. He asked the one in the wrong, "Why are you hitting your fellow Hebrew?" (Exod. 2:13).

The man said, "Who made you ruler and judge over us? Are you thinking of killing me as you killed the Egyptian?" (v. 14).

Moses realized what he had done was widely known. Pharaoh was out to kill him, and his fellow Hebrews mocked him. So he failed and he bailed.

Moses fled to a place called Midian, married a gal named Zipporah, and joined the family business taking care of sheep. The next time we see Moses, forty years have passed; he is now eighty years old . . . and he is stuck.

Moses was stuck in Midian and held hostage by his failures. He had settled for less than what he was made for. Less than what God had prepared him for. Less than what he had hoped for in himself. And there he stayed.

This is where many people drive their tent stakes into the ground and settle. They make a mistake, fall flat on their face, and run away to the far side of the wilderness, hoping no one will notice, praying everyone will just leave them alone, but at the same time absolutely miserable that life has morphed into a monotonous, lackluster checklist. Like Moses, many bury their hopes and dreams to protect their hearts from further disappointment.

God Called Out

Moses was on the far side of the wilderness. And, friend, sometimes it is only on the far side of the wilderness where God can get our attention. Sometimes it is when we feel alone, abandoned, and forgotten that our ears are pricked to hear. Isolation is often God's place of invitation.

Now that you know the backstory, let's join Moses at his wake-up call.

> Now Moses was tending the flock of Jethro his father-in-law, the priest of Midian, and he led the flock to the far side of the wilderness and came to Horeb, the mountain of God. There the angel of the LORD appeared to him in flames of fire from within a bush. Moses saw that though the bush was on fire it did not burn up. So Moses thought, "I will go over and see this strange sight—why the bush does not burn up."
>
> When the LORD saw that he had gone over to look, God called to him from within the bush, "Moses! Moses!"
>
> And Moses said, "Here I am." (Exod. 3:1–4)

Let's hit the pause button for a second. Here's something interesting about this encounter: when God spoke, He didn't speak through a fragrant rosebush, a blooming rhododendron, or a genteel hydrangea. God spoke through a prickly, gnarly, thorny, dried-up, old desert *tumbleweedish* shrub. Oh yes, when God chooses to speak through something or someone, any old bush will do. I don't know about you, but that gives me great hope!

Did you notice *when* God began to speak? "When the LORD saw that he had gone over to look." When God saw that He had Moses's attention, He began to speak. I wonder how many times

I've missed God's gentle whisper and tender tug because I wasn't paying attention. How many times God has tried to speak to me, but I was too busy being busy to notice. Moses turned aside. God spoke.

"Do not come any closer," God said. "Take off your sandals, for the place where you are standing is holy ground." Then he said, "I am the God of your father, the God of Abraham, the God of Isaac and the God of Jacob." At this, Moses hid his face, because he was afraid to look at God.

The LORD said, "I have indeed *seen* the misery of my people in Egypt. I have *heard* them crying out because of their slave drivers, and I am *concerned* about their suffering. So I have come down to *rescue* them from the hand of the Egyptians and to bring them up out of that land into a good and spacious land, a land flowing with milk and honey—the home of the Canaanites, Hittites, Amorites, Perizzites, Hivites and Jebusites. And now the cry of the Israelites has reached me, and I have seen the way the Egyptians are oppressing them." (Exod. 3:5–9)

This was sounding good to Moses! (And it sounds good to me!)

God sees!

God hears!

God is concerned!

God will rescue!

I imagine Moses's heart was pounding, his pulse was quickening, his neck hairs were prickling. Hope was rising! This was great news! Until the next few words rocked his world.

So now, go. *I am sending you* to Pharaoh to bring my people the Israelites out of Egypt. (Exod. 3:10)

Can't you see Moses backing away from the bush . . . holding up his hands as in, "Whoa. Hold on here. You've got the wrong man for the job."

His exact words were, "Who am I that I should go to Pharaoh and bring the Israelites out of Egypt?" (v. 11).

Every insecurity in Moses's emotional storehouse rose to the surface. And in his fainthearted and halfhearted objections, we discover answers to what keeps us stuck in milquetoast faith—what keeps us from moving forward to the land flowing with milk and honey, what keeps us from experiencing the wall-tumbling, giant-slaying, mountain-moving, lame-man-leaping, blind-man-seeing, loaves-and-fishes-multiplying, thriving faith. With each one of Moses's objections and God's answers, we lay a stepping-stone out of the land of stagnant faith and into the land of bold believing, replete with moments of sudden glory when God makes His presence known.

Moses was stuck in the muck and mire of inferiority, insecurity, and inadequacy. He allowed his past failure to stand in the way of his future success. His measuring stick had gotten him stuck as he saw others as more qualified, sanctified, and fortified to do anything meaningful for God. He had lost his confidence, and God was about to show him how to get it back. But this isn't just Moses's problem; it is a potential problem for you and me as well.

Who Am I That I Should Go?

Did you notice that before God told Moses what He was going to do, He reminded Moses who *He* was? "I am the God of your father, the God of Abraham, the God of Isaac and the God of Jacob."

Then Moses replied, "Yeah, I got that. I know who You are, but who am I?"

That question is one of the most important you will ever ask. Your answer will affect the way you look at life, tackle your troubles, and frame your circumstances. The answer to that question will determine your destiny. It can give you the confidence to accomplish your calling or take away your courage to even begin. If you don't answer that question with the truth of God, the devil will answer it for you with his bag of lies.

What do you think ran through Moses's mind when God said, "So now, go. I am sending you to Pharaoh"? I imagine his life flashed before his eyes and he saw all the ways he had disappointed people in his past, not to mention the way he had disappointed himself. *You've got to be kidding! I am a murderer! I am a coward! I am a dirty rotten scoundrel! I am a wanted man! I am so messed up, used up, and fed up! No. No. No. You've made a mistake. You've got it all wrong. You've got the wrong man for the job.*

How many times have I reacted similarly to Moses? Perhaps you have too. As soon as God reveals what He has planned for you to do, the devil reminds you of your past failures and missteps. And I'm not talking about just the mistakes you made before you came to Christ but also the ones you've made since you came to Christ. The times you did *not* flee from temptation but walked right into it, did *not* hold your tongue but lashed out in anger, did *not* wait on God but rushed in to take matters into your own hands. Those are the mistakes the enemy really likes to throw in your face.

And we ask the questions:

Who am I that I should go to Pharaoh?
Who am I that I should write a book?
Who am I that I should start a business?
Who am I that I should start a ministry?
Who am I that I should be a teacher?
Who am I that I should help orphans overseas?
And God replies, "You are who I say you are."

You Are Who God Says You Are

As I mentioned in chapter 1, I became a Christian when I was fourteen. But the feelings of inferiority, insecurity, and inadequacy clung to me like a spider's sticky web. The dirge of "I'm not good enough" was a song I couldn't get out of my head. The lies of the enemy created limitations in my life. They were the barbed wire that fenced me in and kept God's best at bay.

Jesus broke the chains that set the captive free, but as Beth Moore wrote, "Many of us still carry them in our hands or have them dangling from our necks out of pure habit, lack of awareness, or lack of biblical knowledge."[1] I wore those chains like the devil's bling for all three reasons: pure habit, lack of awareness, and lack of biblical knowledge.

The problem was, I didn't really know the answer to Moses's question: *Who am I?* I had no idea who I was, what I had, or where I was as a child of God. Oh, I understood that I was going to go to heaven when I left this earth, but what I was supposed to do until I got there had me stumped. I felt that I was always disappointing God, and I was certainly a disappointment to myself. I tried the best I could to be the best I could be, but I always fell short.

Eventually, I joined the ranks of thousands of Christians before me who settled in the land of in-between. I was saved from my Egypt—the penalty of sin in the hereafter. But I was but worlds away from my Promised Land—experiencing the abundant life in the here and now. I settled into a stagnant faith, a safe faith, the stuck faith with other defeated believers who falsely saw themselves through a filter of past sins and failures rather than through the lens of their new identity as a child of God.

After high school I went to college, where I met and married an amazing Christian man. About four years later, I became a mom. Life was good, except for this termite-like gnawing in my gut that I just didn't quite measure up to all the other church moms with their smiling faces. I walked around with the fear that one day I would be found out—that one day folks would figure out that I wasn't all I was cracked up to be. I lived under an undefined, self-imposed standard of approval.

Childhood echoes of "You're so ugly" and "What's wrong with you?" and "You can't do anything right" left me feeling congenitally flawed. I sat in Bible study groups like someone in a hospital waiting room: hoping for the best but expecting the worst. My greatest fear was that I'd be no closer to being free of the insecurity than I was before the study began.

When I was in my midthirties, I sat under the teaching of an older woman in my church, Mary Marshall Young. She opened my eyes to the truths in Scripture about who I was, what I had, and where I was (my position) as a child of God. I had read those verses scattered throughout Scripture before, but when she encouraged me to cluster them all together into one list, God began a new work in my heart.

You are a saint.

You are chosen.

You are dearly loved.

You are holy.

These truths were right there on the pages of my Bible in black and white and a few in red.

You are reconciled through Christ's life.

You are justified by Christ's blood.

You are free from condemnation through Christ's death.

You have the mind of Christ.

You can do all things through Christ.[2]

I knew the verses were the infallible Word of God, but I felt rather squeamish hearing them, reading them, believing them.

They didn't feel right.

They didn't sound right.

They made me downright uncomfortable.

And all the while I was studying about my true identity, the devil taunted me with accusations. Who do you think you are? A saint? Are you kidding? This stuff might be true about some people, but it certainly is not true about you.

One day God asked me an important question—one He is asking you right now. Who are you going to believe?

I was at a crossroads, one where you might be standing this very moment. Was I going to believe God and begin seeing myself as God saw me, or was I going to continue believing the lies of the enemy and the echoes of my past? Was I going to remain stuck in a stagnant faith because I was too insecure to take a step toward the abundant life Jesus had promised, or was I going to march confidently around the walls of my inadequacies until they came tumbling down?

Finally, I was sick and tired of being sick and tired. "God, I'm going to believe I am who You say I am," I prayed. "I don't feel it. I can barely think it. But I'm going to believe Your Word is true for me and about me."

Have you noticed that it is easier to believe what God says about Himself than what God says about you? Jesus said, "I am the light of the world" (John 8:12). We read those words and shout, "Amen! Hallelujah! Woo hoo!" But He also said, "*You* are the light of the world" (Matt. 5:14). Hmmm. Not a lot of shouting going on with that one. So which is it? Both! Are you going to believe what Jesus said is true about you?

Marketing expert and author Seth Godin wrote, "People don't believe what you tell them. They rarely believe what you show them. They often believe what friends tell them. They always believe what they tell themselves."[3] So start today. Tell yourself the truth and watch God begin to change the way you think.

I am reminded of the exchange between Peter and Jesus when they first met. After Andrew realized he had found the Messiah, he ran to get his brother Peter. Andrew brought Peter to Jesus, and something happened that did not happen with any of the other disciples. Jesus looked Peter in the eyes and said, "'You are Simon son of John. You will be called Cephas' [which, when translated, is Peter]" (John 1:42). "[Simon] means, literally, 'listening,' 'reed-like' or 'grass-like,' hinting perhaps at his human weakness and how easily he was swayed by 'wind of the world.'"[4]

Then Jesus told him who he would be—Peter, which means "rock." He did not cease to be Simon, but Jesus made him something more, something stronger, something better. He revealed his new God-given destiny and purpose. And every time we hear the name Peter in the New Testament, we are reminded that Jesus named him that—Jesus made him that.

Throughout the Gospels, sometimes he is called Simon and sometimes he is called Peter. And I think of you and me. Sometimes I act like my old self, Simon, and sometimes I act like my new self, Peter. But either way, it doesn't change the fact that Jesus has given me a new name and a new identity.

You Are a New Creation

The Bible says, "Therefore, if anyone is in Christ, he is a new creation; the old has gone, the new has come!" (2 Cor. 5:17 NIV 1984). You are not a cleaned-up version of your old self; you are a new creation that did not exist before.

In his book *Victory over the Darkness*, Neil Anderson wrote:

Being a Christian is not just a matter of getting something; it's a matter of being someone. A Christian is not simply a person who gets forgiveness, who gets to go to heaven, who gets the Holy Spirit, who gets a new nature. A Christian, in terms of your deepest identity, is a saint, a spiritually born child of God, a divine masterpiece, a child of light, a citizen of heaven. Being born again transformed you into someone who didn't exist before. What you receive as a Christian isn't the point; it's who you are. It's not what you do as a Christian that determines who you are; it's who you are that determines what you do.

Understanding your identity in Christ is absolutely essential to your success at living the Christian life. No person can consistently behave in a way that's inconsistent with the way he perceives himself. If you think you're a no-good bum, you'll probably live like a no-good bum. But if you see yourself as a child of God who is spiritually alive in Christ, you'll begin to live in victory and freedom as he lived. Next to a knowledge of God, a knowledge of who you are is by far the most important truth you can possess.[5]

John stated in a nutshell why Jesus came: "The reason the Son of God appeared was to destroy the devil's work" (1 John 3:8). Jesus came to set you free—to unlock the shackles of inferiority, insecurity, and inadequacy by equipping you with the power of the Holy Spirit, by lavishing you with precious promises, and by enveloping you in His love. He came to give you a new identity as a child of God.

He came to set you free *from* the shackles of sin and *for* the purposes of God in the here and now. And you have been! Don't let anyone (including yourself) tell you any differently. "It is for freedom that Christ has set us free. Stand firm, then, and do not let yourselves be burdened again by a yoke of slavery" (Gal. 5:1).

The devil wants you to believe you are a no-good, worthless excuse for a Christian who has no power, no victory, and no joy. He knows you have been set free by the blood of Christ, and he will try everything he can to keep you from believing it and walking in it. He'll capitalize on every hurt, magnify every mistake, and punctuate every promise with a question mark rather than a period. He tries to hoodwink you into thinking you're no different than you were before you came to Christ. He's lying.

You are not simply a sinner saved by grace, holding on and doing the best you can until you leave earth or Jesus comes back. You are a dearly loved child of God, a holy saint, and God's workmanship.

A saint? Yes, a saint. That does not mean you are perfect, but it does mean you have been set apart for holy use. That concept was so important to Paul that almost every time he wrote a letter to the New Testament churches, one of the first things he would say was, "You are a saint."

You might read these words and think, *Well, I don't feel like a saint.* I'd say the crippling word in that statement is *feel.* Oh, friend, don't get stuck on a feeling! Let go of the feelings of inferiority, insecurity, and inadequacy and take hold of who you are, what you have, and where you are in Christ. Your true identity is not based on what you have achieved in this life but what you received through Christ's death and resurrection.

You are who God says you are, whether or not you feel like it. However, the way you see yourself will determine the way you live. It is up to you to relentlessly protect your identity and not allow the thief to steal your confidence, which he will try to do every chance he gets.

Believing What You Know

I saw a bumper sticker once that read, "God said it. I believe it. That settles it." But the truth is, God said it and that settles it, whether we believe it or not. His Truth is *the* Truth, and our decision to believe or not believe that Truth does not change its validity. However, it is only through *believing* the Truth that we will *experience* the power of the Truth.

Jesus said, "You will know the truth, and the truth will set you free" (John 8:32). The Greeks had many words for our one word *know.* The Greek word used here is *ginosko.* In the New Testament, it frequently indicates a relationship between the person "knowing" and the object known. It is not just head knowledge of the truth but believing the truth and applying it to your life in action. "There is a sense in which true knowledge (of God) leads to action in keeping with obedience."[6]

All those accumulated verses about my identity in Christ were not new to me when I made my initial list. Perhaps they were not new to you either. I had read them scattered throughout Scripture before and had even memorized a few. But I didn't truly believe them. Not really. I would have never admitted that to anyone—not even to myself. I'd smile and say amen with the best of them. But when the rubber of the truth hit the road of adversity, I moved those verses into the category of nice gestures on God's part rather than the truth that could set me free and give me victory to overcome.

Jesus said this about the Pharisees: "You study the Scriptures diligently because you think that in them you have eternal life. These are the very Scriptures that testify about me, yet you refuse to come to me to have life" (John 5:39–40). These guys studied the Scriptures in minute detail. They knew the Scriptures inside and out, every jot and tittle, dot and dash. However, they did not believe the truth that would have set them free and given them eternal life—the Truth that was standing right in front of them.

Paul wrote to the Ephesians, "And you also were included in Christ when you heard the word of truth, the gospel of your salvation. When you *believed*, you were marked in him with a seal, the promised Holy Spirit" (Eph. 1:13). When you believed in Christ, you were saved from the penalty of sin and you were sealed by the Holy Spirit. *Believed* is a past tense verb, a completed action. Your dead spirit came to life, God forgave you of your sins, and you received a promise of heaven to come.

Now let's read a little farther. Paul continued, "I pray that the eyes of your heart may be enlightened in order that you may know the hope to which he has called you, the riches of his glorious inheritance in his holy people, and his incomparably great power for us who *believe*. That power is the same as the mighty strength he exerted when he raised Christ from the dead and seated him at his right hand in the heavenly realms" (Eph. 1:18–20). You were saved when you *believed*—past tense. You have great power when you *believe*—present tense. Believe what? When you believe God is who He says He is and that you are who God says you are. When you believe the promises of God, the power of God, and the provision of God in your life. When you not only know the truth but believe the truth.

The Greek word for *believe* used in Ephesians 1:19 is a present active participle. That means it is a continuous action verb. "In other words, the promise given in verses 18–20 is not applied to those 'having believed' as in verse 13 where they had believed to become Christians. Rather, it is applied to those who are presently, actively, and yes, continually believing God."[7]

If you feel your walk has become a crawl or your fire for God is a smoldering ember, perhaps what will reignite your passion is a decision to believe what God said is true *for* you and *about* you. Just because God spoke a promise does not mean you automatically possess the promise. You must let go of unbelief and take hold of the promise with the grip of belief to make it yours.

The Bible says you have been given great power through the person of the Holy Spirit. But God's power is only potential power in your life until you convert it to actualized power—when you move forward in obedience and trust.

Every time God reveals a new truth, you must choose to take action. First, you receive the truth into your mind: you know it. Second, you receive that truth into your heart or will: you believe it. Third, you adjust your life to the new truth: you act on it.

God often speaks to me in the newspaper comics—which is a little unnerving. The *Pickles* comic strip features an older couple named Earl and Pearl Pickles. One day Earl and Pearl were sitting on a porch swing and the following conversation ensued:[8]

And there you have it! In the wise words of Earl Pickles, our problem is that we don't really believe everything we know. We go to Bible studies year after year, hear sermons Sunday after Sunday, and read books page after page. But until we move from knowing to believing, we're going to be stuck in the mediocre, mundane, milquetoast faith that expects little and receives even less.

The devil will do anything and everything he can to keep you from believing the truth. Make no mistake about it, he knows you are a chosen, holy, dearly loved child of God who has been created to fulfill a great purpose that God has planned for you. He knows it, and he hates it. His goal is to keep you from believing it. And if he can keep you from believing the truth about your new identity, then he has won. True confidence comes when the words God speaks *about you* become more real *to you* than the lies you've believed all your life.

We will always have a choice to believe the God who made us (fearfully and wonderfully, I might add) or believe the deceiver who wants to hold us hostage in the "less than" mentality. Change always begins with a choice.

The voice you believe will determine your destiny, whether you remain in the land of in-between or venture toward the land of milk and honey—the exciting, adventurous life in Christ brimming with miracles, wonders, and life to the full. Identity always comes before activity. Before you can effectively do what God has called you to do, you must take hold of who God has called you to be.

We need to learn how to overpower the lies of the enemy with the promises of God, and we're going to start right here, right now, by believing the truth about our new, born-again identity. Many of us are driven by a scarcity mentality and see ourselves through the lens of our pre-Christ, spiritually dead existence rather than our born-again, spiritually alive and empowered identity. We are held hostage by the idea that we will never be good enough, though Jesus clearly tells us that, through Him, we already are.

Just before Jesus began His earthly ministry, He traveled to the Jordan River to be baptized by his cousin John. As soon as he came up out of the water, the heavens opened, the Spirit descended, and God spoke: "This is my Son, whom I love; with him I am well pleased" (Matt. 3:17).

Before Jesus performed the first miracle, preached the first sermon, or called the first disciple, God made sure His identity was clear. He was accepted, approved, and completely loved.

So many Christians are trying to earn an acceptance and approval that Jesus has already earned for them. God's acceptance of you is not based on your performance. That doesn't mean we stop trying to do our best to live a God-honoring life. But it does mean we stop trying to earn acceptance we already have. You have nothing to prove because you have already been approved through the finished work of Jesus on the cross and His presence in you.

Allow God to baptize you in the affirmation of your true identity. You are His child, whom He loves. With you He is well pleased.

One More Name

For almost forty years, Marjorie lived with word-inflicted wounds that nearly destroyed her life. From the first day she attended her one-room schoolhouse, she and her teacher, Ms. Garner, didn't get along. Ms. Garner was harsh, bitter, and cruel and could not tolerate Marjorie's childish idiosyncrasies. For years, the tension between the two built up pressure.

Marjorie was nine years old when the cataclysm occurred—and ripped her world apart. It happened after recess when she frantically raced into class, late again. As she burst through the doors, she faced her peers glaring at her.

"Marjorie!" Ms. Garner shouted. "We have been waiting for you! Get up here to the front of the class, right now!"

Marjorie walked slowly to the teacher's desk, was told to face the class, and then the nightmare began.

Ms. Garner ranted, "Boys and girls, Marjorie has been a bad girl. I have tried to help her to be responsible. But apparently she doesn't want to learn. So we must teach her a lesson. We must force her to face what a selfish person she has become. I want each of you to come to the front of the room, take a piece of chalk, and write something bad about Marjorie on the blackboard. Maybe this experience will motivate her to become a better person!"

Marjorie stood frozen next to Ms. Garner. One by one, the students began a silent procession to the blackboard. One by one, the students wrote their life-smothering words, slowly extinguishing the light in Marjorie's soul. "Marjorie is stupid! Marjorie is selfish! Marjorie is fat! Marjorie is a dummy!" On and on they wrote until twenty-five terrible scribblings of Marjorie's "badness" filled the chalkboard.

The venomous sentences taunted Marjorie in what felt like the longest day of her life. After walking home with each caustic word indelibly written on her heart, she crawled into her bed, claiming sickness, and tried to cry the pain away. But the pain never left, and forty years later, she slumped in the waiting room of a psychologist's office, still cringing in the shadow of those twenty-five sentences.

After two long years of weekly counseling, Marjorie finally began to extricate herself from her past. It had been a long and difficult road, but she smiled at her counselor (how long it had been since she'd smiled!) as they talked about her readiness to move on.

"Well, Marjorie," the counselor said softly, "I guess it's graduation day for you. How are you feeling?"

After a long silence, Marjorie spoke. "I . . . I'm okay."

The counselor hesitated. "Marjorie, I know this will be difficult, but just to make sure you're ready to move on, I am going to ask you to do something. I want you to go back to your schoolroom in your mind and detail the events of that day. Take your time. Describe each of the children as they approach the blackboard; remember what they wrote and how you felt—all twenty-five students."

In a way, this would be easy for Marjorie. For forty years, she had remembered every detail. And yet, to go through the nightmare one more time would take every bit of strength she had. After a long silence, she began the painful description. One by one, she described each of the students vividly, as though she had just seen them, stopping periodically to regain her composure, forcing herself to face each of those students one more time.

Finally, she was done, and the tears would not stop, could not stop. Marjorie cried a long time before she realized someone was whispering her name. "Marjorie. Marjorie. Marjorie." She looked up to see her counselor staring into her eyes, saying her name over and over again. Marjorie stopped crying for a moment.

"Marjorie. You . . . you left out one person."

"I certainly did not! I have lived with this story for forty years. I know every student by heart."

"No, Marjorie, you did forget someone. See, He's sitting in the back of the classroom. He's standing up, walking toward your teacher, Ms. Garner. She is handing Him a piece of chalk and He's taking it, Marjorie, He's taking it! Now He's walking over to the blackboard and picking up an eraser. He is erasing every one of the sentences the students wrote. They are gone! Marjorie, they are gone! Now He's turning and looking at you, Marjorie. Do you recognize Him yet? Yes, His name is Jesus. Look, He's writing new sentences on the board. 'Marjorie is loved. Marjorie is beautiful. Marjorie is gentle and kind. Marjorie is strong. Marjorie has great courage.'"

And Marjorie began to weep. But very quickly, the weeping turned into a smile, and then into laughter, and then into tears of joy.[9]

For forty years, Marjorie had limped through life with the pain of a broken heart. She had been held hostage by those twenty-five sentences. But finally she allowed Jesus, the Healer, the Comforter, the Great Physician, to heal her broken heart and set her free.

Lies also held our friend Moses hostage for forty years. It wasn't quite forty years for me, but pretty close.

What about you? Are you ready to overpower the lies of the enemy with the truth of God? Here's what Jesus is writing on the chalkboard about you:

- You are chosen.
- You are dearly loved.
- You are holy.
- You are beautiful.
- You are pure.
- You are My bride.
- I have your name engraved on the palm of My hand.
- You are My child, whom I love; with you I am well pleased.

three

You've Got What It Takes

Let Go of the Scarcity Mentality
and Take Hold of Abundant Promises

Did you notice God's answer to Moses's first question, "Who am I that I should go to Pharaoh?" Let's go back to the burning bush and take a look. We'll back up a few verses to keep it all in context.

The LORD said, "I have indeed seen the misery of my people in Egypt. I have heard them crying out because of their slave drivers, and I am concerned about their suffering. So I have come down to rescue them from the hand of the Egyptians and to bring them up out of that land into a good and spacious land, a land flowing with milk and honey—the home of the Canaanites, Hittites, Amorites, Perizzites, Hivites and Jebusites. And now the cry of the Israelites has reached me, and I have seen the way the Egyptians are oppressing them. So now, go. I am sending you to Pharaoh to bring my people the Israelites out of Egypt."

But Moses said to God, "Who am I that I should go to Pharaoh and bring the Israelites out of Egypt?"

Now let's go a bit farther and ponder God's reply.

And God said, "*I will be with you.* And this will be the sign to you that it is I who have sent you: When you have brought the people out of Egypt, you will worship God on this mountain." (Exod. 3:7–12)

When Moses asked, "Who am I that I should go to Pharaoh?" God had an unusual reply. It was almost as if He ignored the question on the table and told Moses what he really needed to know.

"I will be with you."

In other words, "Don't worry about who *you* are. Concentrate on who *I* am. I'll be with you. I've got this. You just hang on tight."

Isn't it a comfort to know God is always with you? Always! David wrote:

> Where can I go from your Spirit?
>> Where can I flee from your presence?
> If I go up to the heavens, you are there;
>> if I make my bed in the depths, you are there.
> If I rise on the wings of the dawn,
>> if I settle on the far side of the sea,
> even there your hand will guide me,
>> your right hand will hold me fast.
>> Psalm 139:7–10

Paul wrote:

> For I am convinced that neither death nor life, neither angels nor demons, neither the present nor the future, nor any powers, neither height nor depth, nor anything else in all creation, will be able to separate us from the love of God that is in Christ Jesus our Lord. (Rom. 8:38–39)

The writer of Hebrews reminds us that God's words to the Israelites also apply to you and me:

Never will I leave you; never will I forsake you. (Heb. 13:5; see also Deut. 31:6, 8; Josh. 1:5)

God's presence envelops us as we live and move and have our being in Him. So many times we glibly suggest or imploringly beg for God to be with us as if we have to coax Him out of hiding. David debunks that idea. There is no place we can go that is away from God's presence. Most Christians would say they believe this truth, but many then live like they don't.

One day I was praying for my son, a prayer that had almost become as rote as "God is great. God is good." "God, please be with Steven today," I whispered.

Just as abruptly as a referee's whistle calling foul, God stopped me mid-sentence. *Why do you pray that every day?* He seemed to say. *I am with Steven. I'm with him every day. Why do you ask for something he already has as if you don't believe Me?*

God was right! Imagine that. So I amended my mother prayer. "Dear Lord, please help Steven be aware of Your presence today."

The truth of God's here-ness and nearness is punctuated throughout Scripture. "If you feel far from God, guess who moved?" was a common saying back in the 1980s. But God is not a being who can be moved away from. There is nowhere you can go that is away from His presence. But (and this is a big *but*) you can *feel* far from God. The cure for the *feeling* of farness comes in capsules of praise, thanksgiving, and acknowledgment of His presence. It comes in practicing the presence of God.

The good news is that practicing the presence of God is not as arduous as learning to play a musical instrument or as physically taxing as preparing for a marathon. Practicing the presence of God is found in acknowledging His presence in all of life—in the boardroom, the bedroom, and everywhere in between. It is simply a two-step, danced to the rhythm of God's cadence, in the spin of the laundry and the sizzle of bacon in the pan. Practicing the presence of God is the constant awareness of His presence and the attentive acknowledgment of His workings.

All of us feel closer to God at some times more than others. But it is just a feeling. (Don't get stuck on a feelin'.) The truth is, I feel closer to my husband at some times more than others. But that doesn't mean I'm any less married at some times than others. I usually feel closer to him after we've enjoyed a fun time together, been especially intimate, or gone through a struggle in which we've locked arms and walked through it together.

It's not that much different in my relationship with God. I might feel closer to Him when we've had a good time together (as in worship), been especially intimate spiritually (as in a morning quiet time), or gone through a struggle in which we've locked arms and walked through the difficulty together (as in mourning the death of a loved one).

But just because I feel closer to God in a particular moment doesn't mean I am. It's just a feeling. A wife cannot have that giddy feeling about her spouse all the time. Likewise, we cannot have that giddy feeling about God all the time.

We will always feel far from God when we ignore Him, live independently from Him, or rush about expecting Him to tag along. And while your humanness wavers between spiritual times of plenty and times of want, the feeling of nearness to God is always just a whisper away as you acknowledge His presence with you and in you.

Yes, what a joy and a comfort to know there is nowhere we can go that is away from God's presence. He will never leave us or forsake us. The fact that we live in His presence makes every moment of life meaningful. He is in our moments and our moodiness, our days and our dalliances, our weeks and our weaknesses. If only we would notice.

When the Lord saw that Moses had turned aside to look—He spoke.

A Big Move

We have the same promise of God's presence that He gave Moses at their fireside chat: "I will be with you." But here's the real kicker— you've got something even more than Moses ever dreamed of. You have Jesus *in* you. He doesn't stop by for an occasional visit. He's moved in to stay. Paul wrote, "I have been crucified with Christ and I no longer live, but Christ lives in me" (Gal. 2:20).

I don't mean to sound like the man on the infomercial, but that's not all! There's more! Not only do you have Jesus in you, but you are also in Jesus. For every one time the New Testament mentions that Jesus is in you, there are ten that say you are in Him. Ten to one!

The night before Jesus's arrest, He explained to His disciples, "I will not leave you as orphans; I will come to you. Before long, the world will not see me anymore, but you will see me. Because I live, you also will live. On that day you will realize that I am in my Father, and you are in me, and I am in you" (John 14:18–20).

Being "in Christ" can be a difficult concept to visualize. Perhaps that's why the church has focused on Christ in the believer rather than the believer in Christ, even though Scripture has it quite the other way around.

Here's an exercise that helps me visualize this concept. I hope you'll try it. Write Jesus's name on a little card and place that card in an envelope. Write your name on that envelope. There you have Jesus in you.

Now take that envelope and put it in a larger envelope. Write Jesus's name on the larger envelope. Now you have Jesus in you and you in Jesus.

Finally, place all of that in an even larger envelope and write "God" on the outside. Now you have Jesus in you, you in Jesus, and all that in God. "On that day you will realize that I am in my Father, and you are in me, and I am in you" (John 14:20). "In

Christ" is your new address—it is where you live. As real estate agents often say, when it comes to determining the value of a piece of property, location is everything. Your location in Christ deems your worth beyond measure.

The realization of Jesus in you will give you the security, peace, and confidence to tackle any task God calls you to *do* or any situation He calls you to *go through*. The power and authority that accompany that position have the potential to lift your boat from the sandbar of mediocrity and set your sails to capture the wind of the adventurous faith.

When you were born *physically*, the Bible says you were born "in sin" or "in Adam." When you were born again *spiritually*, you were re-born "in Christ." The principle that the believer is "in Christ" is one of the major themes of the New Testament. In the little book of Ephesians alone, Paul states forty times that the believer is "in Christ."

And when did this change occur? The moment you believed. God took you out of Adam and placed you into Christ. A person is either "in Adam" or "in Christ." We don't have the option to *not* be in one or the other. But we do have a choice as to which one we will be "in."

This is not simply a good idea for how we should live or how things ought to be. It is the truth of your position as a child of God right now . . . today. It's all about location, location, location.

You may not have realized when the switch occurred, or even *that* it occurred when you came to Christ. You most likely didn't *feel* the change. But be sure of this: God said it and it's true. The fact that you are *in Christ* is a present reality, not a future hope.

You may not always be conscious of being in Christ any more than you are conscious that you are in your bed when you're asleep. When I lay my head on the pillow at night, I am fully aware that I am in my bed. When I fall asleep, I am not aware that I am in my bed, but I am still there. I may not be conscious of the fact that I am in Christ at all times—I may not feel anything different. But that does not change the fact that I am in Christ as I live and move and have my being in Him.

Jesus did not say, "Come to me and abide *with* me." He said, "Abide [or remain] in me" (see John 15:1–10).

So what does all this have to do with getting unstuck from cul-de-sac Christianity, to moving beyond the land of in-between? Everything. When I think of Jesus in me, I picture Him going where I'm going—always with me. That's a comfort. But when I think of me in Jesus, I picture me going where He's going. That's exciting! That's the adventurous faith! That's life to the full! I can't see Jesus pulling up a lawn chair, propping up His feet, and settling down under a shade tree, growing soft and bored. And I can't see myself doing that either.

Jesus said, "This is the work (service) that God asks of you: that you believe in the One Whom He has sent [that you cleave to, trust, rely on, and have faith in His Messenger]" (John 6:29 AMPC). *The work*, as Jesus calls it, is to believe, to trust. At first glance that seems fairly easy. Like being the backseat rider on a tandem bicycle and resting your feet on the handlebars while the driver does all the peddling. But I haven't met anyone yet who relinquishes control and completely trusts with ease. Trusting, resting, and giving up control go against our natural bent. But isn't our natural bent what Jesus came to save us from?

Paul wrote, "But whoever is united with the Lord is one with him in spirit" (1 Cor. 6:17). Jesus doesn't want us to simply follow after Him. He wants us to live in union with Him. I believe there is a big difference. *"In* him we live and move and have our being" (Acts 17:28), not behind Him. And when this verse becomes a reality in our lives, we will experience a bold faith that will help us take hold of the promises of God and move forward in maturity and action.

An Exciting Ride

My son was just a preschooler when I first taught him to snow ski. The very first day was arduous—for me. I felt like a down-covered workhorse as I lugged two sets of skis in one arm while dragging along Steven with the other. Clunky ski boots, overstuffed mittens, and a hooded snowsuit made it difficult for Steven to maneuver. Add all that to the slippery snow, long lift lines, and a resistant four-year-old, and you have the makings of a windfall of whining in a winter wonderland.

After several failed attempts to teach Steven how to snowplow down the bunny slope with the ski tips pointed inward, I came up with another idea. I made an A-frame tent with my legs. Then Steven stood in front of me with his arms wrapped around my thighs, and off we went! He went where I went. If I moved right, he moved right. If I moved left, he moved left. His only responsibility was to hang on and relinquish control.

"I'm skiing! I'm skiing!" he shouted as we sped down the slope.

And even though he thought he was skiing, in reality he was simply along for the ride.

What a picture of how I want my journey with Jesus to be! I cling to Him, wrap my arms around Him, and move where He moves. If He goes left, I go left. If He goes right, I go right. "But the person who is joined to the Lord is one spirit with him" (1 Cor. 6:17 NLT). We are in Him and He is in us. And I can promise you this: when we move in tandem with Jesus, we're in for the ride of our lives! And God was getting Moses ready for his.

A Rich Inheritance

Unless you are a baseball fan, married to one, or a mom to one, you probably haven't heard of Matthew Joseph White. He signed with the Cleveland Indians in 1998, the Boston Red Sox in 2002, and the Colorado Rockies in 2003. But it is not his baseball career that captured my attention.

In 2003, Matt had an aunt who needed to go into a nursing home. She didn't have the funds to make the move, but she did have a piece of land in his home state of Massachusetts. So Matt agreed to pay her $50,000 for the forty-five acres of mountain real estate, which gave her enough to enter the nursing home and get the care she needed.

Matt's original intent was to build a home on the property, but he found the ground too hard. When he called a surveyor to inspect the acreage, he discovered treasure lying beneath the rocky soil. The land was solid Goshen stone, a type of valuable mica. Approximately twenty-four million tons of mica schist rock, worth about $100 per ton, had been resting on the mountain for thousands of years. The estimated worth of Matt's land? Two point five billion dollars.

When my husband read me Matt's story in a sports magazine, my mind immediately went to the truth of what we have in Christ. Most of us are sitting on a mountain of precious promises and don't even know it. Goshen stone may be valuable, and I am tickled pink that Matt made the discovery. But followers of Christ are sitting on a treasure worth even more. Jesus is the Rock, and God has already paid the excavation costs. The title deed has your name on it, and you simply need to take hold of it to access your glorious inheritance.

Precious Promises

Being in Christ comes with many benefits. You are a dearly loved, completely accepted, totally forgiven, uniquely chosen child of God. And because you have been adopted into God's family, you are now heir to a plethora of precious promises.

For starters, when you exhale your last breath on earth, you will inhale heaven for all eternity. No other promise comes close in comparison. But there's more, so much more. That's what we're excavating in the pages of this book.

Paul wrote, "What we have received is not the spirit of the world, but the Spirit who is from God, so that we may understand what God has freely given us" (1 Cor. 2:12). So stop and pray with me for just a moment. "Dear Lord, I pray that You will open my mind to comprehend all that You have given me. Help me to let go of preconceived notions and small-minded thinking to take hold of all that You have for me. In Jesus's name, amen."

Did you pray? Did you mean it? Let's keep going! As you read the following words, take note of the verb tense in each sentence.

Praise be to the God and Father of our Lord Jesus Christ, who *has blessed* us in the heavenly realms with every spiritual blessing in Christ. For he *chose* us in him before the creation of the world to be holy and blameless in his sight. In love he *predestined* us for adoption to sonship through Jesus Christ, in accordance with his pleasure and will—to the praise of his glorious grace, which he *has freely given* us in the One he loves.

In him we have redemption through his blood, the forgiveness of sins, in accordance with the riches of God's grace that he *lavished* on us. With all wisdom and understanding, he *made known* to us the mystery of his will according to his good pleasure, which he *purposed* in Christ, to be put into effect when the times reach their fulfill-ment—to bring unity to all things in heaven and on earth under Christ.

In him we *were also chosen*, having *been predestined* according to the plan of him who works out everything in conformity with the purpose of his will, in order that we, who were the first to put our hope in Christ, might be for the praise of his glory. And you also *were included* in Christ when you heard the message of truth, the gospel of your salvation. When you believed, you *were marked* in him with a seal, the promised Holy Spirit, who is a deposit guaranteeing our inheritance until the redemption of those who are God's possession—to the praise of his glory. (Eph. 1:3–14)

Did you see it? Paul is describing blessings and promises you already have. Every single one of those verbs is in past tense. You don't need to earn these blessings and promises. You don't need to wait for them. You simply need to take hold of what is already yours. You've already got what it takes to live bold.

God made the deposit in your safe-deposit box before the creation of the world, fashioned the key in the shape of a cross, and gave you access the moment you believed. Far too many of us leave the blessings sitting in the vault gathering dust.

When it comes to believing the promises of God, most tend to approach it as if they were sitting in a sterile waiting room hopeful and afraid, longing for a good report but expecting the worst. Here's the truth of the matter: "His divine power has given us everything we need for a godly life through our knowledge of him who called us by his own glory and goodness" (2 Pet. 1:3). Everything? Everything. God has given you everything you need to live the victorious, abundant, fulfilling, vibrant life in Christ. That doesn't mean life will be easy. Jesus said, "In this world you will have trouble" (John 16:33). But it does mean God has given you everything you need to do and to go through whatever He has purposed for you.

God didn't save you and then put you on the front lines and say, "Now do the best you can." He has given you everything you need to live the life He has called you to live. He has given you the power of the Holy Spirit, the mind of Christ, the riches of heaven . . . just to name a few.

Shared Inheritance

When my husband, Steve, was in high school, he worked various jobs and was notoriously frugal. His twin brother, Dan, and their best friend, Mike, were not quite as thrifty. Dan and Mike had odd jobs from time to time—flipping hamburgers at the Wild Pig being the most infamous. But their funds disappeared as quickly as they got them. Steve, on the other hand, was a saver. And they knew it.

Steve had a little brown wallet with a horse head on the front and a zipper on the top. It was his "saving wallet," and he kept it safely tucked away in his sock drawer. Occasionally, Steve, Dan, and Mike would get together to plan an adventure, such as a weekend trip to the beach or the mountains, or just a wild night out on the town playing putt-putt. Dan and Mike would often say, "Let's just pool all our money together. Steve, go get your horse head. We'll put all our money on the table and combine it. We won't worry about whose is whose."

They knew Mr. Thrifty would have about thirty dollars to match each of their one-dollar contributions. It was a great deal for them. Not so much for Steve.

When we come to Christ, it is as though Jesus says, "Just put what you have in with what I have. Let's make one big pot. What's Mine is yours."

The Bible says you are a co-heir with Christ (Rom. 8:17). That means you get what Jesus gets. You didn't earn this inheritance. God is not giving it to you because you were particularly good. He has lavished you with blessings because it pleases Him to do so (Eph. 1:5).

When will you receive this inheritance? You already have! Notice the verb tense in Ephesians 1:11: "In him we have obtained an inheritance" (ESV). You *already have* obtained it. It is simply up to you to know it, believe it, and act on it.

The Holy Spirit abides in all believers. You've already been given everything you need to live victoriously in and through all things. And yet we wonder—at least I do—*Why don't I operate in the power I already have? Why is my love so fickle? My power so pale? Why do I cower rather than make demons flee? Why do I live in the cul-de-sac of Christianity rather than venture out on the highways and byways of the adventurous faith?*

I believe living bold comes with practice. First, you know the truth. You know it, right? Second, you believe the truth. I don't mean just believe it is true but believe it is true for you and in you. Third, you act on it, walk in it, stomp about in the surefootedness of it.

God does not need to be stirred, prodded, or roused as if from a sound sleep. We do. We need to wake up, take hold, and live in the power that is already ours.

No matter what you are going through today or will go through tomorrow, your destiny is greater than your difficulty, greater than your dilemma, greater than your discouragement. And God has given you everything you need to get there.

John wrote, "What great love the Father has lavished on us, that we should be called children of God!" (1 John 3:1). To *lavish* is to give freely, profusely, extravagantly, and abundantly. He doesn't give us everything we want when we want it. No father wants spoiled children. Rather, He gives us everything we need to become well-behaved children who bear His name well.

Another translation of 2 Peter 1:3 says God has "granted to us everything pertaining to life and godliness" (NASB). The word *granted* paints the picture of transferring something from one person to another. And isn't that exactly what God did for you? He transferred these precious promises from His heart right into your account—not because you deserved them or earned them but because of His magnificent grace. And notice the verb tense of the word *granted*. It is past tense. It has already been done. This is not something you will receive in the future; you have access to His promises right here, right now.

It's Personal

Aren't you excited to know that God has deposited rich blessings and a lavish inheritance into your account? Tell me, what reason do we have to feel inadequate? In light of what we have in Christ, I can't think of a thing. But how do we access these magnificent promises? Peter says, *"Through our knowledge of him* who called us by his own glory and goodness" (2 Pet. 1:3).

As I mentioned earlier, the Greeks had several words for the word *knowledge*. The one used here is *epignosis*. This is a strengthened form of the word and implies a larger, more thorough, and intimate knowledge. It is not simply knowing something intellectually but understanding and believing what you know in a personal way.[1]

When Steve and I traveled to Ephesus, a local tour guide took us through the landmarks, ruins, and history of the early church. She knew the facts about Christianity and more about the dates, locations, and nuances of Paul's visits than we did. When we stopped for lunch, I asked her if it would be okay with her if we asked God to bless our food. She bowed her head with us as we prayed. When she opened her eyes, she said, "Thank you. I've never experienced that before."

This Turkish woman knew about Christianity, but she had no *epignosis* of Jesus. She knew all about the historical aspects of the religion, but she did not know the One who came to set her free.

Even demons know who Jesus is—and they shudder (James 2:19). The devil knows exactly who Jesus is, what He has done, and what He will do in the final days. But the devil does not know Him experientially as Savior and Lord. Paul says that through knowing Jesus intimately, personally, and experientially, we have everything we need—precious and magnificent promises.

Like a tiny baby born to be king, most of us have no idea what those great and mighty promises entail, what our rich inheritance contains, or what our spiritual birthright bestows. As you open the pages of God's Word, He begins to reveal the truth of who you are and what you have as a child of God. And remember, this is not a promise of what you will have one day but of what you have the moment you believe.

These promises are called precious and valuable. I love how the New American Standard Bible translation refers to them as "magnificent promises" (2 Pet. 1:4). The word *magnificent* means "splendid, lavish, beautiful; as to arouse admiration and wonder."[2] And oh how God's magnificent, splendid, lavish, and beautiful promises arouse admiration and wonder of who He is and what He does. Oh my goodness, why in the world would I feel inadequate?! Thickheadedness and unbelief are my only excuses.

And how does He give us everything we need for life and godliness? How does He dole out the precious promises? He gives freely. Pours out lavishly. It costs us nothing. It cost Jesus everything.

Incomparably Great Power

Jesus said, "Very truly I tell you"—don't you just love it when He says that?—"whoever believes in me will do the works I have been doing, and they will do even greater things than these, because I am going to the Father" (John 14:12). Now that is a commission to live bold if I've ever heard one. But how? How do we do that? By relying on the power of the Holy Spirit working in us and through us.

Take a glove, for example. A glove is powerless sitting on a bedside table. But put your hand in the glove and it can do many things: play the piano, paint a picture, scrub a floor, or plant a garden. But is that the glove or the hand in the glove doing the work? Of course, it is the latter.

You and I are nothing more than gloves—powerless on our own, yet powerful when filled with the Spirit. The glove can't do anything if it is merely near the hand. It must be filled with the hand—controlled by the hand. And it is the same for us. We have power to do everything God has called for us to do when we are filled with the power of the Holy Spirit.

Paul prayed that we would believe in and take hold of the truth that we have great power as children of God and co-heirs with Christ. He calls it "incomparably great power" (Eph. 1:19). Immeasurable. Unlimited. Inexhaustible. He doesn't pray that we will *have* more power but that we will *realize* we already have the power. But we must engage the gears to experience that power.

When my husband and I were first married, we purchased a five-speed Honda Civic. It was a snappy silver stick shift with high gas mileage and low horsepower. The conundrum was that I didn't know how to drive a stick shift. Steve gave me a lesson on driving a car with a manual transmission, but I was scared to death to change gears. Step on the clutch. Slowly release while slipping the stick into first gear. Step on the clutch again. Slowly release while slipping the stick into second gear. It was just too much for me to remember.

We lived in Chapel Hill, North Carolina, at the time—the primary word being *hill*. There were lots of hills. When I pulled up to a stop sign at the top of one of those hills and had to do the clutch-gear trick, I panicked. I feared I would roll backward into the car behind me before I could move forward. I was a mess. That was on a Saturday.

The following Monday I had to drive the car to work all by myself. I made it out of the neighborhood and all the way to third gear. However, when I pulled onto the highway with commuters whizzing by, I was too afraid to let off the gas, push in the clutch, and shift into fourth.

First gear. Second gear. Third gear. Even though I knew there were two more gears to go, I was afraid to engage. Third was enough for me. So I drove the poor little Civic twenty miles at highway speed in third gear. It was not good for the car. It was not good for me. When I confessed my wicked ways to Steve, he was not pleased.

Are you driving through life in third gear? I daresay some never get out of first. Some walk the aisle, raise the hand, or perhaps fill out a commitment card, but then they putter along in first gear when their spiritual lives are meant to be driven in fifth. No wonder our engines wear out.

Now listen, we are not meant to slide along in neutral either. Relying on the power of the Holy Spirit does not mean we sit back and do nothing. We have to take hold—to engage the power of the Holy Spirit to do all God has called us to do and be all God has intended us to be.

God can use whatever you've got, but you've got to *use* what you've got. Look what Jesus did with five loaves and two fish. Look what David did with a single stone; look what Shamgar did with the jawbone of an ox. The point is, they used what they had. We tend to pray that God will give us more power. But it could be that He is waiting for us to access the power we already have. Let go of excuses. Take hold of what you have in Christ. Move forward. Live bold.

Suited Up for More

Pretend with me for a moment. Let's say you are on an island in the Pacific. Pick an island, any island, but make it a tropical, lush, and beautiful one. You walk out onto the porch and see some equipment laid out just for you. You know what it is, and you know what it's for. You're excited! You've always wanted to do this but never had the right gear.

You slip into a sleek, black wet suit, zip up the front closure, and most likely marvel at the way it holds everything in. Then you squeeze your feet into squeaky black flippers. I know they're tight, but go ahead and wiggle your feet in. Next, you strap a heavy oxygen tank on your back. One arm. Now the other. Finally, you slip a face mask over your nose and eyes and place a mouthpiece between your lips.

But rather than heading out to the ocean to explore the marvelous coral reef, vibrantly colored fish, and swaying flora, you turn around, go back into the house, fill up the bathtub, and settle in.

What a silly picture. If I were there with you, I think, I'd march right into that bathroom and say, "What are you doing in that tub? Get out there in the ocean where you belong!" But then I remember I have done the very same silliness time and time again.

So many of us are equipped to live the abundant life in Christ but don't even know it. We suit up but then settle in. We resign ourselves to living the mediocre faith void of vibrancy, wonderment, and awe. Don't head to the bathtub with your scuba equipment on. Head out to the ocean of preordained opportunity and experience all God has for you. You've already got the gear. It's just up to you to jump in.

Moses had everything he needed to accomplish the task God had preordained for him to do. He was saved by Pharaoh's daughter, raised in Pharaoh's house, trained in the Egyptians' ways, and taught the Egyptian language. He "was powerful in speech and action" (Acts 7:22). But he had forgotten. God was about to jog his memory.

four

The God Who
Fills In Your Gaps

*Let Go of Feelings of Inadequacy
and Take Hold of God's All-Sufficiency*

All my adult life I had been a wife and a mom with several other hats thrown into the mix. But when my son was in middle school, I had an inkling all that was about to change. Not the wife and mother part, but the other hats, the other dabblings. I had written a few Bible studies and taught several more. I had scribbled a handful of *sudden glory* life lessons learned on holy field trips and stuffed them in a metal drawer. That's where the stories stayed—stuck in between my files on appliance warranties and tax returns.

Then one day I opened the drawer and noticed the swelling file had become multiple files. Hundreds of stories and studies bulged from green hanging file folders begging to be set free. They seemed to have grown overnight, but the truth was, they had multiplied while I wasn't paying attention. I began to pray about what God would have me do with all these scribblings, if anything.

One year after I first uttered the prayer, I met a gal who was starting a parachurch organization called Proverbs 31 Ministries. She invited me to join her on our local radio station to record a few short segments featuring ten of my stories. When we finished, she turned to me and said, "Sharon, I have been praying for one year that God would send me a ministry partner to take over radio and help me with the running of Proverbs 31. I think God is telling me you are that person."

"That's nice, Lysa," I replied. "But I don't know anything about radio and running a ministry. I think you've got the wrong person. But I'll pray about it."

I had no intention of saying yes. Nice Christian girls in the South always say they're going to pray about something when they have every intention of saying no. My plan was to say no after the respectable amount of time had passed.

But you know what? I did pray about it. I struggled with that list of verses about my new identity in Christ posted on my refrigerator door. I read them with more of a question mark at the end than a period. The three-headed monster of insecurity, inferiority, and inadequacy reared its ugly head with taunts, and I began to question everything I supposedly believed. I argued with God. I identified with Moses.

- Who am I that I should go?
- I'm not smart enough.
- I'm not talented enough.
- I'm not good enough.
- I can't talk in front of groups.
- I can't write.
- Shoot, I can't even spell.

- I sound too Southern.
- I don't know anything about radio.
- I don't have a theology degree.
- I don't know anything about running a 501(c)(3) organization.

I'm not, I can't, I don't, and *I never will* flew in the face of my newly discovered identity in Christ. I was Moses at the burning bush arguing with God—questioning the wisdom of it all. I was fully aware I was not practicing what I had been preaching, and I had a decision to make.

Two weeks into my hissy fit with God, Steve suggested a romantic vacation to the island of Bermuda—a paradise off the coast of Cape Hatteras, North Carolina. On one particular evening, we splurged at a fancy restaurant, complete with a four-man band playing music from the forties and fifties. We had taken a scant few ballroom dance classes, and Steve was itching to see if we could remember the foxtrot.

"Come on, Sharon," he urged. "Let's take a spin on the dance floor."

"No way," I said. "Nobody else is dancing. I'm not going to be the only one out there with everyone staring at me. And suppose we mess up? I'd be embarrassed. It's been a long time since we've practiced, and I don't remember all the steps. Let's wait until there are some other people out there so we won't be so conspicuous."

After a few moments, the first couple took their place on the parquet. They squared their shoulders, pointed their toes, and framed their arms. In one fluid motion they graced the dance floor with perfect dips, sways, turns, and twirls. They looked good, and they knew it.

Nope. I was not going to embarrass myself tonight. I hunkered down in my seat with renewed resolve. I refused to budge.

Then couple number two joined couple number one. Their steps weren't quite so perfect, but they looked pretty good too.

"Okay, I'll go," I said. "But let's get in the back corner behind that big ficus tree so nobody can see us."

And off we went to try to remember the slow-slow-quick-quick of the foxtrot. The whole time I was hoping all the audience members were still mesmerized by the polished artistry of couple number one.

As I dared to look at the crowd, I noticed they were not looking at couple number one, number two, or even wobbly kneed number three. All eyes were fixed on a fourth couple approaching the dance floor. You see, the husband was in a wheelchair.

He was a middle-aged, slightly balding, large-framed man with a neatly trimmed salt-and-pepper beard. His dapper attire included a crisp white shirt, a snappy bowtie, and a stylish tuxedo. On his left hand he wore a white glove—I guessed to cover a skin disease. With a smiling wife by his side, he approached the dance floor with a graceful confidence and fashionable flair. Suddenly everyone else faded away, and they seemed to be the only two people in the room.

As the band churned out a peppy tune, the blithesome wife held her love's right hand and danced. He never rose from the wheelchair that had become his legs, but they didn't seem to care. They came together and separated like expert dancers. He spun her around as she stooped low to conform to her husband's seated position. Lovingly, like a little fairy child, she danced around his chair while her laughter became the fifth instrument in the musical ensemble. Even though his feet never left their metal resting place, his shoulders swayed in perfect time and his eyes danced with hers.

My heart was so moved by this love story unfolding before my eyes that I had to turn my head and bury my face in Steve's jacket so no one would see the tears streaming down my cheeks. As I did, I saw person after person dabbing linen napkins to dewy eyes. This portrait of love and devotion transfixed even the misty-eyed band members.

Finally, the music slowed to a romantic melody. The wife pulled up a chair beside her husband's wheelchair but facing in the opposite direction. They held each other in a dancer's embrace, closed their eyes, and swayed back and forth, cheek to cheek.

Surprisingly, I no longer worried about whether anyone was watching me. I didn't care if my steps weren't perfect. I wasn't even concerned about being compared to and falling short of perfect couple number one.

The Lord spoke to my heart in a powerful way. Yes, there was a burning bush right smack-dab in the middle of the dance floor.

Sharon, I want you to notice—who moved this crowd to tears? He seemed to say. *Was it couple number one, with their perfect steps? Or was it the last couple, who had no steps at all? No, My child, it was the display of love, not perfection, that moved the crowd. If you obey Me, if you do what I have called you to do, then I will do for you what that man's wife did for him.*

God reminded me that He is not looking for perfect people with perfect children, perfect marriages, and perfect lives. He is not searching for men and women with perfect steps to do great things for Him. He is looking for courageous believers who will rely on His power to work in and through them to accomplish all He has planned for them to do. He is scouting for followers who will obey Him regardless of their present fears or past failures. He reminded me of His words to Moses: *I will teach you what to say. I will show you what to do.*

Simply put, God had sent a lame man to teach me how to dance.

I Am Is the God Who Is

Are you ready for the next stepping-stone on the path to moving beyond the land of in-between? To moving beyond the stagnant faith of the wilderness and venturing into the thriving adventurous faith of the Promised Land? I can hardly wait! Let's join Moses where we left him, still arguing with God by the burning bush. We'll back up a few steps to keep the conversation in context.

"So now, go. I am sending you to Pharaoh to bring my people the Israelites out of Egypt."

But Moses said to God, "Who am I that I should go to Pharaoh and bring the Israelites out of Egypt?"

And God said, "I will be with you. And this will be the sign to you that it is I who have sent you: When you have brought the people out of Egypt, you will worship God on this mountain."

Moses said to God, "Suppose I go to the Israelites and say to them, 'The God of your fathers has sent me to you,' and they ask me, 'What is his name?' Then what shall I tell them?"

God said to Moses, "I AM WHO I AM. This is what you are to say to the Israelites: 'I AM has sent me to you.'. . . Say to the Israelites, 'The LORD, the God of your fathers—the God of Abraham, the God of Isaac and the God of Jacob—has sent me to you.' This is my name forever, the name you shall call me from generation to generation." (Exod. 3:10–15)

"I AM." Moses must have thought that a strange name for God. It sounds like the bush's reception was breaking up a bit. "God, I heard the first part of Your answer but not the last. I got the I AM part, but I AM who? I AM what?"

"You heard me right," God replies. "I AM WHO I AM. This is what you are to say to the Israelites: 'I AM has sent me to you.'"

I AM. He was. He is. He always has been. He always will be. He is the Self-Existent One with no beginning and no end. J. I. Packer, in his book *Knowing God*, states, "He is: and it is because He is what He is that everything else is as it is."[1]

God has many names in the Bible, and each name reveals a unique aspect of His character and His ways—who He is and what He does. Our finite human minds can barely scratch the surface of the depth of His wisdom, the breadth of His love, the magnitude of His power, or the height of His grace. He is Elohim, the Creator; El Roi, the God Who Sees; El Shaddai, the All-Sufficient One; Yahweh-Yireh, the Lord Will Provide; Yahweh-Rapha, the Lord

Who Heals, just to name a few. Like the beauty of a multifaceted diamond, each name reveals a new depth of insight to be explored.

When God revealed His name, I AM, He did so using a present tense Hebrew verb—an action word. He is a God who acts on His people's behalf. He is a God who acts on *your* behalf.

In *Knowing God by Name*, I wrote:

> God uses two forms of the same name in this passage. I AM is the name He refers to when speaking of Himself. LORD, or Yahweh in the Hebrew, is the third person form of the word and translated "He is." When God speaks of Himself, He says, "I AM," and when we speak of Him, we say, "He is."
>
> Originally, the Name was only four letters: YHWH. Later, scribes inserted vowels to form the word Yahweh. Some Bible translations render the same name as Jehovah. YHWH appears in the Old Testament more than 6,800 times, and is found in every book except Esther, Ecclesiastes, and the Song of Songs. When you see the name LORD in all caps in the Bible, it is referring to Yahweh. When you see the word Lord in lower case, it is referring to another name for God—Adonai.
>
> The Name YHWH was considered so holy to the early rabbinical scribes, they wouldn't even write the letters. They used "The Name," "The Unutterable Name," "The Great and Terrible Name," and "The Holy Name" whenever it appeared. You can imagine the Pharisees' surprise when Jesus said, "Very truly I tell you . . . before Abraham was born, I AM!"[2]

Jesus echoed God's words of Exodus 3:14 and in those two little words expressed the eternity of His being and His oneness with the Father. Jesus, who is the exact representation of God's character and His ways (John 14:8–9; Heb. 1:3), went on to make seven other I AM statements. He is the bread of life who sustains you (John 6:35), the light of the world who guides you (John 8:12), the gate who opens heaven for you (John 10:9), the shepherd who cares for you (John 10:11–14), the resurrection and the life who gave His life for you (John 11:25), the way, the truth, and the life who offers abundant life on earth and eternal life hereafter to you (John 14:6), and the vine who supplies your every need (John 15:1, 5).[3]

I AM says it all. He just is. Before there was anything, HE WAS. The Scriptures begin with the words, "In the beginning God" (Gen. 1:1). He always has been and always will be.

I AM points to the very present tenseness or the *is-ness* of God—the *here-ness* and *nearness* of God. *He is* your very present help in times of trouble. The writer of Hebrews tells us, "And without faith it is impossible to please Him, for he who comes to God must believe that He is and that He is a rewarder of those who seek him" (Heb. 11:6 NASB).

Moses was eighty years old when he had his argument with God at the burning bush. But what we'll see is that in the hands of I AM, even the weakest knees become a mighty force to be reckoned with.

I AM Is the God Who Fills In Your Blanks

I'll go out on a limb and say that every single one of us, at one time or another, will struggle with feelings of inferiority, insecurity, and inadequacy just like Moses did. And the underlying statement feeding the sense of worthlessness is I'm not _____ enough. You can fill in that blank with any number of qualities.

I'm not strong enough.

I'm not experienced enough.

I'm not talented enough.

I'm not brave enough.

I'm not pretty enough.

I'm not thin enough.

I've written an entire book on seventy-five of the most common "I'm not _____ enough" statements and lies women believe that hold them hostage to feelings of inferiority, insecurity, and inadequacy, and I barely scratched the surface.[4]

But here's what I want you to remember: whatever you feel you are not, God is. Whatever you need, God is. He is the God who fills in your gaps; He is I Am who fills in your blanks.[5]

Once we let go of the lies that we are not enough and take hold of the truth that we are more than enough because of Jesus's presence and power in us, then we will be set free from the mealymouthed mentality and be on our way to experiencing the courageous confidence of an overcomer.

Here's what I want you to do: I challenge you to "spot the nots" in your self-assessment as you go about your day. Sleuth for the "I am nots" in your thoughts and in your speech. For example, look out for words spoken or thoughts such as *I'm not smart enough*; *I'm not pretty enough*; *I'm not good enough*. Then once you "spot the not," I want you to "swat the not." That's right. Swat it right out of your vocabulary. Here's the deal: whenever you say, "I'm not _____ enough," God says, "I Am."

When You Say	God Says
I am not smart enough.	I Am
I am not talented enough.	I Am
I am not patient enough.	I Am
I am not loving enough.	I Am
I am not caring enough.	I Am
I am not wise enough.	I Am
I am not strong enough.	I Am
I am not outgoing enough.	I Am
I am not secure enough.	I Am
I am not bold enough.	I Am
I am not _____ enough.	I Am

Now go back and read that list again. But this time, read it out loud. Go ahead. Nobody's watching. If they are, they'll be blessed too.

After I published a blog post on this topic, Julie wrote the following to me:

> I just recently began a new job for the second part of my life. I am fifty-two and decided that if I was going to work, I wanted it to be fun. So after working sixteen years as an intervention aide in public schools, I switched to a child development center. I didn't realize how hard it would be to leave my comfort zone. It is hard to begin again and learn new things. At the same time, my dad had open-heart surgery, my father-in-law went into hospice care, and my mother-in-law experienced a fall, which ultimately ended her journey here on earth. I often feel overwhelmed with all that needs to be done to close up my in-laws' home and balance a full-time job. But God is the God who fills in my blanks. He is everything I need. When I say, "I am not strong enough to keep doing this," God says, "I AM." When I say, "I'm not brave enough to go through my in-laws' things," God says, "I AM." Thank you for the reminder.

"Nots" swarm like flies on the unaware and unsuspecting. Let me encourage you to spot the nots in your life. Hunt them down. Sleuth them out. Spot them. And once you spot the nots, swat the nots right out of your mind. Get rid of them. If you have a pen in your hand right now, go back to that list and put a big X right through those nots.

I AM is the God who is everything you need. He is the God who fills in your blanks.

I AM Is the God Who Fills In Your Gaps

In the first *Rocky* movie, the Italian Stallion, Rocky Balboa, very eloquently encouraged his demure girlfriend, Adrienne: "I got gaps. You got gaps. Together we got no gaps."

But Rocky got it all wrong. He's got gaps. Adrienne's got gaps. And no person alive is going to fill in those gaps. God is the only One who can fill in our gaps. And I'd go so far as to say that He is the One who gave us those gaps so He *can* fill them. He is the great I Am who fills in our gaps and fills in our blanks. I've often heard it said there is a God-shaped vacuum in the heart of every human being that cannot be filled by another created thing but only by God, the Creator, made known through Jesus Christ.

Paul wrote, "[God] said to me . . . My strength and power are made perfect (fulfilled and completed) and show themselves most effective in [your] weakness" (2 Cor. 12:9 AMPC).

Paul knew what he could accomplish on his own: nothing. Oh, he could be busy. We all can do that. But bearing "fruit that will remain" is another story. This is how he viewed his own personal weaknesses:

> I was given the gift of a handicap to keep me in constant touch with my limitations. Satan's angel did his best to get me down; what he in fact did was push me to my knees. No danger then of walking around high and mighty! At first I didn't think of it as a gift, and begged God to remove it. Three times I did that, and then he told me,
>
> > My grace is enough; it's all you need.
> > My strength comes into its own in your weakness.
>
> Once I heard that, I was glad to let it happen. I quit focusing on the handicap and began appreciating the gift. It was a case of Christ's strength moving in on my weakness. Now I take limitations in stride, and with good cheer, these limitations that cut me down to size—abuse, accidents, opposition, bad breaks. I just let Christ take over! And so the weaker I get, the stronger I become. (2 Cor. 12:7–10 Message)

Paul had great confidence. The prefix *con* means "with," and the root *fid* means "faith." So a confident person is one who walks in faith. When you allow God to fill in your gaps with His power and provision, you will have the confidence and courage to leave the limpid land of in-between and march into the Promised Land of life to the full!

I Am Is the God Who Calls You to More

Gideon, like Moses, settled into a stymied faith and stagnant existence. His goal was to survive, but certainly not to thrive. Gideon was among the second generation Israelites who had marched into the Promised Land. But then because of fear of the Midianites, he, along with the rest of the Israelites, hid among clefts and caves rather than enjoy the land God had given them.

One day Gideon was threshing wheat in a winepress. Any farmer knows you don't thresh wheat in a winepress. You thresh wheat out in the open field so the grain will fall to the ground as the wind blows away the chaff. But cowardly Gideon was threshing wheat in a winepress because he was afraid of those testy Midianites.

Suddenly, an angel of the Lord appeared and addressed Gideon: "The LORD is with you, *mighty warrior*" (Judg. 6:12). Mighty warrior? Can't you just see Gideon looking around and saying, "You talkin' to me?" (I smell a burning bush here.)

God addressed Gideon as "mighty warrior" not because he was one but because He knew what Gideon could be if he trusted in God's power to work in him and through him. He knew what Gideon could be if he allowed I Am to fill in his gaps.

As for you, my friend, God has this to say: You are more than a conqueror through Jesus Christ who loves you (Rom. 8:37). He has given you the victory through our Lord Jesus Christ (1 Cor. 15:57). You can do all things through Christ who gives you strength (Phil. 4:13). You are a mighty warrior (even if you do wear cute shoes).

He is the God who fills in your gaps . . . especially when He calls you to more than you think you are able to do.

I Am Is the God Who Works Miracles

Lisa was a girl who partied every chance she could get. She was a bartender. A cocktail waitress. A fun-lovin' girl without a care in the world . . . until one day the stick turned blue.

Lisa had grown up in a Christian home and walked the aisle when she was eight years old. But in her twenties, Lisa had put Jesus up on a shelf so she could live the wild life. Then in 1996, she discovered she was pregnant, and her fast-paced world came to a screeching halt.

After several home pregnancy tests, Lisa decided she needed an "official" test from a medical facility. She got in her car and headed to the abortion clinic where she had gotten her contraceptives. She knew they would encourage her to have an abortion, and frankly, she was committed to continuing her partying lifestyle with as little interruption as possible. But on the way to the clinic, something happened. God happened.

Lisa saw a two-story brick building with a sign that read, "Charlotte Pregnancy Care Center." She felt as though God was beckoning her, wooing her, drawing her to pull into the parking lot. She did. I'll let Lisa tell you what happened in her own words:

> I remember it just like it was yesterday. From the moment I got out of my car, I just felt like the Lord was with me. I walked into the center and was met by a woman with a nice, warm, and caring smile. Not a smile that was a "I'm just doing my job" smile, but a caring smile.
>
> She came over, met me, introduced herself, and put her hand on my arm. "You have come to the right place," she said. "We're here to help."

I felt like I had just walked into the arms of Jesus. The love, the compassion, the confidence and sensitivity in her voice were incredible. She wanted to know about me. We talked and she listened. She was gentle and kind.

We discussed how I felt and what I wanted out of life. What I wanted for me and for my *baby*. She called it a "baby." Not "a pregnancy" like so many do in the early stages of pregnancy. She confirmed that my test was positive and gave me a due date.

I remember hearing her words and the Holy Spirit using those words to tell me it was going to be okay, but that I would have to change.

A week or two went by, and this woman called to check on me and to ask how I was doing. I thought, *Wow—this is amazing. She really cares!*

Lisa decided not to have an abortion but to carry this child to term. A few weeks later she went to the doctor for her first prenatal visit.

On my first prenatal visit, the doctor did an ultrasound. "Lisa, I have some bad news," he began. "There is a problem with your uterus. The embryo has connected to a part of your uterus where there is a separation. It will not live. Your body will not be able to carry to term. You can easily abort at this stage and get back to your normal life. This does not have to be an interruption."

But as he was talking, I was listening. I was listening to him, but I was also listening to a voice in my right ear that was saying, "It's going to be fine. You are going to be fine." I even asked my mom, who was with me, if she heard it too. She didn't. The voice was just for me.

The doctor left the room for a moment, and when he came back in, I looked at him and said, "I'm not having an abortion. I'm having my baby."

Well, Lisa did have her baby, a girl. Jordan Reese Holt was born weighing 7 pounds, 5 ounces, and measuring 20 inches long. Perfectly healthy. Magnificently beautiful.

In the fall of 2012, Charlotte Pregnancy Care Center celebrated its thirtieth anniversary. They had planned a celebration banquet with Bruce Wilkerson as the speaker. For a year, the staff had prayed for just the right testimony to share. As soon as the announcement about the banquet went up on their website, Lisa called to order a ticket.

"The center has meant so much to me," she began. "I came to the center seventeen years ago on my way to an abortion clinic . . ."

Lisa told the receptionist the story just as I told you and ended her conversation with these words: "My daughter, Jordan, just turned sixteen, and we want to celebrate by coming to the banquet."

With tears streaming down her cheeks, the receptionist ran into the director's office and said, "Erin, I think I just found the testimony for the banquet."

Lisa met with Erin at a restaurant, told her the story, and showed her pictures of Jordan today. Then she said, "By the way, I saved a slip of paper from the center that the counselor gave me that day—the one that confirmed I was pregnant. I keep it in Jordan's baby book. Would you like to see it?"

"Yes, I'd love to," Erin replied.

Lisa slid the slip of paper across the table for Erin to see. At the bottom was scribbled the name of the counselor: *Sharon Jaynes*.

I was the counselor that day.

Oh, friend, when Erin emailed me this story, I cried for four days. I am not kidding. Of all the babies saved over the past thirty years at that one center, God put His hand in the hat and pulled out this story just for me, and for you.

I am not telling you this to get a pat on the back. I am telling you because of how God helped me spot the not, swat the not, and answer His call at a time when I wanted to do anything *but* be at a pregnancy care center.

Here's what you need to know: When I felt God calling me to be a counselor at the center, I did not want to go. *No! No! No!* I inwardly cried. I had gone through years of struggling with second-ary infertility. Not being able to have children or losing a child due to miscarriage, stillbirth, or untimely death can be one of the most heart-wrenching experiences of a woman's life. The inner turmoil associated with infertility is a raw wound that scabs over and opens up with each passing month. I had miscarried a much-prayed-for child, and the pain was still fresh, the grief was still heavy. And now God was calling me to volunteer at a place where most of the clients did not want their children.

"No way, God," I complained. "This is too much. This is too hard. I don't want to do it! I'm not qualified. I'm not emotionally strong enough."

A whole slew of "nots" flung wild. To be honest, I was a little bit ticked off at God.

But God was persistent and consistent. He knew facing my pain head-on would bring healing. So I asked God to write His name in my blanks, to fill in my gaps with His grace, my deficiency with His sufficiency, and my weakness with His strength. I walked in obedience, even though I didn't feel like it.

A second thing I want you to know is this: When Erin told me the story of Lisa and how God used me to encourage her to carry her baby to term, I didn't remember it happening. I didn't remember Lisa. I didn't remember what I had said to her or anything else about that day. But Lisa did. And that is the beauty of allowing God to work through you. You can't take the credit. All I did was show up.

Sometimes God will call you to step out of the ordinary into a great adventure—a work He has planned for you to do (Eph. 2:10). You may not want to do it. You may feel you are not smart enough, talented enough, strong enough, or bold enough. You may argue with God like Moses did (Exod. 3–4). You may laugh at God like Sarah did (Gen. 18:12). You might want to run like Jonah did (Jon. 1:3). You might hide like Saul did (1 Sam. 10:22). But if you obey God and depend on I AM to fill in your gaps, amazing things will happen. People will be blessed. You will be blessed. Lives will be changed, and the greatest change may be in you.

We may never know the people who are blessed by our obedience to speak a word, to lend a hand, or to give a hug. We may never know the lives that are impacted by our obedience to do what God has called us to do. But we can know this—there will be low-hanging, abundant fruit with your name on it—if you allow God to fill in your gaps! Miracles happen when you let go of your perceived inadequacies, take hold of God's all-powerful sufficiency, and move forward in faith.

Even today I keep a picture of Jordan on my cell phone to remind me of what can happen when a child of God lets go of the hindrances that hold her hostage and takes hold of the promises of God to act, to be, to do all He has purposed.

five

The Freedom of Forgiveness

*Let Go of Crippling Bitterness
and Take Hold of Radical Forgiveness*

So far we've taken an in-depth look at Moses's first objection to God's call on his life, "Who am I that I should go?" and discovered our true identity in Christ. We've explored Moses's second objection with his question to God, "What is your name?" and taken solace in the truth that the great I Am is the God who fills in our gaps. Now let's ponder Moses's third objection and discover how God's response will help us let go of the hindrances that hold us hostage and take hold of the promises that set us free.

After God revealed His name, I Am, He gave Moses further instructions:

> Go, assemble the elders of Israel and say to them, "The Lord, the God of your fathers—the God of Abraham, Isaac and Jacob— appeared to me and said: I have watched over you and have seen

what has been done to you in Egypt. And I have promised to bring you up out of your misery in Egypt into the land of the Canaanites, Hittites, Amorites, Perizzites, Hivites and Jebusites—a land flowing with milk and honey." (Exod. 3:16–17)

What if they do not believe me or listen to me and say, "The LORD did not appear to you"? (Exod. 4:1)

What if they do not believe me or listen to me? Where did Moses come up with that notion? I'll tell you where. He reached back forty years and remembered. He had already tried to help the enslaved Hebrews forty years earlier, and they did not listen to him or believe him. Moses could have said, "Suppose they don't believe me or listen to me like they didn't forty years ago? I've already tried to rescue these people once, and look where that got me!"

And now God was asking him to go back to the same people who had mocked him with the words, "Who made you ruler and judge over us?" The same people who had rejected him, belittled him, and turned their noses up at him. The same people who had hurt his heart . . . and Moses didn't want to have anything to do with them.

I know how he felt. I wonder if you do too. I wonder if people in your past have hurt you, abused you, or misused you. People who belittled you, mocked you, or hurt your heart. What do we do with those crippling emotions? How do we break free of the bitterness, hurt, and resentment that hold God's best at bay? There's only one way.

Held Hostage by Unforgiveness

I was stuck and didn't know what to do. I was praying. God was silent.

After high school, I moved ninety miles away and attended a community college for two years. I earned a degree in dental hygiene and then returned to my hometown to work for two wonderful dentists. Most of my friends were still away at college, and I was terribly lonely. After the first year of working in a dental practice, I had an urge to go back to school and further my degree. I prayed but felt no direction or clarity. Not to decide is to decide, so I continued at my current job.

When the second spring came around, my desire to return to school resurfaced. The confusion about what to do and where to go resurfaced as well. At the same time, I began having flashbacks of suppressed, disturbing childhood memories.

In frustration, I went to visit a man who had been a spiritual mentor in my small town. "Mr. Thorp," I cried, "I have been praying for over a year about what to do with my future. I know God has more for me than this. I feel such unrest—an urge to go back to school—but I don't know what to do. I don't have a peace about anything. Can you please pray with me and for me?"

"Is there anything else going on you'd like to tell me about?" he asked.

"Well, I've been having disturbing flashbacks from my childhood. Some nightmares when I sleep and flashbacks during the day." I went on to describe some of the terrifying scenes.

Mr. Thorp decided we should read some Scripture about prayer before we prayed for God's direction.

First he turned to Matthew 6:8–15.

For your Father knows what you need before you ask him. This, then, is how you should pray:

"Our Father in heaven,
hallowed be your name,
your kingdom come,
your will be done,
    on earth as it is in heaven.
Give us today our daily bread.

And forgive us our debts,
    as we also have forgiven our debtors.
And lead us not into temptation,
    but deliver us from the evil one."

For if you forgive other people when they sin against you, your heavenly Father will also forgive you. But if you do not forgive others their sins, your Father will not forgive your sins.

Then he turned to Matthew 18:19–22.

"Again, truly I tell you that if two of you on earth agree about anything they ask for, it will be done for them by my Father in heaven. For where two or three gather in my name, there am I with them."

    Then Peter came to Jesus and asked, "Lord, how many times shall I forgive my brother or sister who sins against me? Up to seven times?"

    Jesus answered, "I tell you, not seven times, but seventy-seven times."

Each time Mr. Thorp turned to a passage about God answering prayer, there was one about forgiveness either before or after it.

    "Sharon," he said, "I sense God is telling you that you have not forgiven your father for things that happened in your childhood. Is that true?"

    I wanted to say, "Wait a minute. I came here to ask for prayer about my future, not about my past." But God was showing me that my refusal to forgive my father for what happened in my past was blocking His work in my future. To move forward, I needed to let go of the residual resentment and take hold of the grace-filled forgiveness.

    That night I forgave my dad for everything he had ever done. When I let go of the bitterness, anger, and resentment, my life moved to a new and deeper level of intimacy with God.

    Miraculously, the next day the cloud of confusion lifted. I applied to college in late spring, even though the head of the department told me it was too late and the program I desired to enroll in was already full. She explained that the only way entry would even be a possibility was if someone was to drop out—"which never happens." Confident that this was God's plan for me, I resigned from my job and found an apartment near the college campus. Ten days before the start of the fall semester, the head of the department called and said, "You won't believe this, but someone just dropped out. We'd like you to come in the fall if you can make the arrangements."

I could believe it and the arrangements were already made. I enrolled in the fall and met my husband four weeks later. The following summer I became his wife.

I am not saying that when you forgive those who have hurt you, you'll strike it rich, find the man of your dreams, or live happily ever after. However, I do believe that refusing to forgive can block God's power in your life and hold you hostage in a "less-than" place other than what God intends.

I was in bondage for many years because of unforgiveness. Hear me on this: it was bondage. I was held captive by it—shackled to it. I put my pain on a pedestal and dusted it off from time to time so I'd never forget. All the while, the key to freedom was right within reach.

What Is Forgiveness?

Paul was a man who had a lot to forgive. He recounted the cruelties and injustices inflicted on him in his letter to the Corinthians:

> I have worked much harder, been in prison more frequently, been flogged more severely, and been exposed to death again and again. Five times I received from the Jews the forty lashes minus one. Three times I was beaten with rods, once I was pelted with stones, three times I was shipwrecked, I spent a night and a day in the open sea, I have been constantly on the move. I have been in danger from

rivers, in danger from bandits, in danger from my fellow Jews, in danger from Gentiles; in danger in the city, in danger in the country, in danger at sea; and in danger from false believers. I have labored and toiled and have often gone without sleep; I have known hunger and thirst and have often gone without food; I have been cold and naked. (2 Cor. 11:23–27)

As I read these verses, I always wonder when and where those things happened to Paul. He made little mention of the hardships and ill treatment throughout the pages of the New Testament. If I had suffered such treatment, I'd probably bring it up often and dedicate a whole chapter to each one! But not Paul. He let go of the past and moved on. In his estimation, the past cruelties and abuses were barely worth mentioning.

Paul had a choice. He could allow what had happened to him to make him bitter or better. He chose the latter. I believe one of the reasons Paul was able to accomplish more than anyone in the New Testament other than Jesus Christ was because of his willingness to let go of offenses and keep moving toward the goal of conformity to the character of Christ.

Paul wrote, "But one thing I do: Forgetting what is behind and straining toward what is ahead, I press on toward the goal to win the prize for which God has called me heavenward in Christ Jesus" (Phil. 3:13–14). This one thing I do—forgetting what is behind.

When Paul writes that he is "forgetting what is behind," that does not mean he is obliterating something from his memory. That is physically impossible unless you have some type of dementia. What he *does* mean is that he is no longer going to allow his past to determine his future. Forgetting was a continual, conscious refusal to let the past absorb his attention and impede his progress. He was committed to let go of the past and take hold of all that Christ Jesus had taken hold of for him.

It is also important to note that the word *forgetting* is a present tense verb . . . a continual action. That means we might have to put the offense behind us today, and then when the devil brings it to our remembrance tomorrow, we put it behind us again. It might work something like this: You may have to forgive someone a hundred times the first day of your resolve, the second day, and even the third. But as time passes, it will require less and less effort until one day you realize you have forgiven completely. While forgiveness is a decisive act of the will, putting the offense behind us, in the biblical sense of forgetting, is a process.

Sometimes a trigger may surface the memory of the offense, an emotional trap door opens beneath your feet, and the hurtful feelings all come back. That doesn't mean you haven't truly forgiven the person. It simply means you need to remind yourself that you already have. Forgiveness cannot be proven by your feelings. It is an act of the will. Hopefully, the feelings will follow, but they don't always.

The Greek word for forgiveness is *aphiemi*, and it means "to let go from one's power, possession, to let go free, let escape."[1] The picture of biblical forgiveness is to cut someone loose. The word picture is one in which the unforgiven is roped to the back of the unforgiving. When we refuse to forgive, we bind ourselves to what we hate. When we forgive, we cut the person loose from our backs and set *ourselves* free.

Forgiveness can also be seen in terms of canceling a debt. In the Old Testament, when someone paid a debt, a notice of the debt paid in full was nailed to the lender's door. That is what Jesus did when He was nailed to the cross—our debt was paid in full and nailed to heaven's door. When you forgive someone, you cancel a debt, which he or she could never repay anyway.

Forgiveness has nothing to do with whether the offender deserves forgiveness. Most do not. I do not deserve God's forgiveness and yet He has forgiven me. It is *not* saying what the person did or didn't do doesn't matter. If it didn't matter, there would be nothing to forgive.

Forgiveness means taking someone off your hook and placing him or her on God's hook. It is cutting the offender loose from your back and giving the burden of justice to God. Forgiveness is no longer allowing the offender to hold you captive by holding a grudge. You don't forgive people because they deserve it but because you need it.

In his book *What's So Amazing about Grace?*, author Philip Yancey said, "If we do not transcend nature, we remain bound to the people we cannot forgive, held in their vise grip. This principle applies even when one part is wholly innocent and the other wholly to blame, for the innocent part will bear the wound until he or she can find a way to release it—and forgiveness is the only way."[2]

Forgiveness is not:

- Saying what the offender did was not wrong
- Saying what the offender did doesn't matter
- Absolving the person from responsibility for his or her actions
- Denying the wrong occurred
- Pretending the abuse did not happen

Forgiveness is:

- Letting go of your need for revenge
- Cutting the person loose from your back and giving the burden to God
- Refusing to let bitterness and hatred rule your life
- Releasing the burden of resentment
- Transferring the administration of justice to God

Forgiveness Walks on Stage

In the book of Genesis, we meet a young man named Joseph—the eleventh of twelve brothers and favorite son of Jacob. He is most famously known for his elaborate coat of many colors. Young Joseph had several prophetic dreams involving his brothers and father one day bowing down to him. Rather than keep that bit of information to himself, he shared it with his already jealous siblings. When he was seventeen, his brothers had enough of this rather bratty brother. So one day, when Joseph went out to the fields to check on them, they schemed to throw him into a well, shred his fancy coat, and tell Jacob his favorite son had been killed by a wild animal. Just after they had tossed him into the pit, an Egyptian caravan came passing by. Then they hatched another plan; rather than leave Joseph to die, they sold him into slavery and pocketed a bit of money in the process.

Joseph served as a slave in the home of a high-ranking official named Potiphar. While there, he was falsely accused of sexually assaulting Potiphar's wife and thrown into prison. During his prison stay, he interpreted dreams for some of his fellow inmates, and God blessed him.

One day the pharaoh of Egypt had a disturbing dream that no one could interpret. Pharaoh's cupbearer, who had been in prison with Joseph, told the king about Joseph's gift of interpretation. Joseph interpreted Pharaoh's dream and predicted seven years of plenty followed by seven years of famine. Pharaoh was so enamored with Joseph's God-given wisdom that he appointed him governor of Egypt, second only to Pharaoh himself.

During the famine, who should show up in Egypt looking for food but Joseph's conniving brothers. They were terrified when the governor revealed that he was their long-lost brother. "I am your brother Joseph, the one you sold into Egypt!" There were tears all around. Can you imagine how scared they must have been? What would Joseph do? What would you do?

This was Joseph's response to the injustice inflicted by his brothers: "Do not be distressed and do not be angry with yourselves for selling me here, because it was to save lives that God sent me ahead of you. . . . You intended to harm me, but God intended it for good to accomplish what is now being done, the saving of many lives" (Gen. 45:5; 50:20).

Pastor Chuck Swindoll notes, "Joseph blazes a new trail through a jungle of mistreatment, false accusations, undeserved punishment, and gross misunderstanding. He exemplifies forgiveness, freedom from bitterness, and an unbelievable positive attitude toward those who had done him harm. He forgave those who had harmed him and made sure bitterness never had a chance to take root."[3]

Joseph did not say to his brothers, "Oh, that's okay. Don't worry about it." No, he called the betrayal what it was—evil against him that resulted in thirteen years of slavery. At the same time, he chose to forgive the wrong done *to* him and allow God's grace to flow *through* him. He opened the door for reconciliation and entrusted the matter of justice to God.

Thus ends the first book of the Bible: Genesis. We close out the epic narrative with a portrait of forgiveness that continues throughout the entire Bible. The word *forgive* walks out on the stage as a leading character for the entirety of the Scriptures, and it begins with the words of Jacob—an elderly father making a request to his wronged son.

> "This is what you are to say to Joseph: 'I ask you to forgive your brothers the sins and the wrongs they committed in treating you so badly.' Now please forgive the sins of the servants of the God of your father." When their message came to him, Joseph wept. (Gen. 50:17)

Forgiveness rewrites the ending to the story. Not only does it ease the pain to make letting go of the past offenses easier, but it also releases the aroma of hope that helps us reach out to the possibilities for the future.

Forgiveness is a continuous theme throughout Scripture, and it all begins with a very mixed-up family—how appropriate. I'm sort of glad. That gives me great comfort.

Setting the Captive Free

Corrie ten Boom was a Dutch Christian who lived during the time of World War II. During that time, her family rescued and hid Jews in their home to help them escape the Nazi Holocaust. Eventually, Hitler's soldiers discovered the family's clandestine activities and hauled them off to prison. Seven months later, Corrie and her sister, Betsie, were herded into boxcars and transported to Ravensbrück, a notorious concentration camp where an estimated 50,000 would breathe their last. The prison built to house 6,000 was crowded with 32,000 by the war's end. Barracks built for 250 women housed 1,000 to 2,000 at a time. Corrie and Betsie lived in a flea-infested barracks under freezing conditions with three or four women to a bed. Starvation, barbaric cruelty, and the stench of death were ever-present reminders of the evil surrounding them. Corrie held her emaciated sister as she died in her arms.

Amazingly, when Corrie ten Boom was released from Ravensbrück at the close of the war, she returned to Holland to set up rehabilitation centers and various charities. During that time, she often spoke about the power of forgiveness. In perhaps one of her most poignant moments, while she was speaking to a church in Munich, her commitment to forgiveness was tested as never before.

And that's when I saw him, working his way forward against the others. One moment I saw the overcoat and the brown hat; the next, a blue uniform and a visored cap with its skull and crossbones. It came back with a rush: the huge room with its harsh overhead lights, the pathetic pile of dresses and shoes in the center of the floor; the shame of walking naked past this man. I could see my sister's frail form ahead of me, ribs sharp beneath the parchment skin. *Betsie, how thin you were.*

The place was Ravensbrück, and the man who was making his way forward had been a guard—one of the most cruel guards.

Now he was in front of me, hand thrust out: "A fine message, Fraulein! How good it is to know that, as you say, all our sins are at the bottom of the sea!"

And I, who had spoken so glibly of forgiveness, fumbled in my pocketbook rather than take that hand. He would not remember me, of course—how could he remember one prisoner among those thousands of women?

But I remembered him and the leather crop swinging from his belt. I was face-to-face with one of my captors, and my blood seemed to freeze.

"You mentioned Ravensbrück in your talk," he was saying. "I was a guard there." No, he did not remember me.

"But since that time," he went on, "I have become a Christian. I know that God has forgiven me for the cruel things I did there, but I would like to hear it from your lips as well, Fraulein." Again the hand came out. "Will you forgive me?"

And I stood there—I whose sins had again and again to be forgiven—and could not forgive. Betsie had died in that place—could he erase her slow, terrible death simply for the asking?

It could not have been many seconds that he stood there—hand held out—but to me it seemed hours as I wrestled with the most difficult thing I had ever had to do.

For I had to do it—I knew that. The message that God forgives has a prior condition: that we forgive those who have injured us. "If you do not forgive men their trespasses," Jesus says, "neither will your Father in heaven forgive your trespasses."

I knew it not only as a commandment of God but also as a daily experience. Since the end of the war I had had a home in Holland for victims of Nazi brutality. Those able to forgive their former enemies were able also to return to the outside world and rebuild their lives, no matter what the physical scars. Those who nursed their bitterness remained invalids. It was as simple and as horrible as that.

And still I stood there with the coldness clutching my heart. But forgiveness is not an emotion—I knew that too. Forgiveness is an act

92

of the will, and the will can function regardless of the temperature of the heart. "Jesus, help me!" I prayed silently. "I can lift my hand. I can do that much. You supply the feeling."

And so woodenly, mechanically, I thrust my hand into the one stretched out to me. And as I did, an incredible thing took place. The current started in my shoulder, raced down my arm, sprang into our joined hands. And then this healing warmth seemed to flood my whole being, bringing tears to my eyes.

"I forgive you, brother!" I cried. "With all my heart."

For a long moment we grasped each other's hands, the former guard and the former prisoner. I had never known God's love so intensely as I did then. But even so, I realized it was not my love. I had tried, and did not have the power. It was the power of the Holy Spirit.[4]

Pastor Brian Zahnd, in his book *Unconditional?*, says this about the gospel: "If Christianity isn't about forgiveness, it is about nothing at all. . . . Christian forgiveness is not cheap. Rather it is costly because it flows from the cross—the place where justice and forgiveness meet in violent collision. Christian forgiveness does not call us to forget. Christian forgiveness allows us to remember but calls us to end the cycle of revenge."[5]

We see what Brian Zahnd tells us displayed so beautifully in Corrie ten Boom's story. In her recounting, she makes some very important observations about forgiveness:

- Forgiveness is not easy.
- Forgiveness is not a feeling.
- Forgiveness is a choice to follow Christ.
- Forgiveness serves as a conduit for the love and power of the Holy Spirit to flow from the one forgiving to the one forgiven.
- Forgiveness is not weakness. It is strength. Any simple-minded sinner can hold a grudge. It takes the power of God to forgive.

• Forgiveness not only sets the offender free but sets the offended free as well.

As I think about this Dutch woman's story, I am reminded of another Dutch word with horrific implications: *apartheid*. It was a legislated system of racial segregation in South Africa from 1948 to 1994 where the 10 percent white population harshly ruled and abused the black majority. Nelson Mandela spent twenty-seven years in prison for his fight against apartheid. When the system was dismantled and Mandela was released from prison, he made a commitment to continue the fight for equality without bitterness. "As I walked out the door toward the gate that would lead to my freedom," he said, "I knew if I didn't leave my bitterness and hatred behind, I'd still be in prison."[6] Mandela's acts of forgiveness for the injustices incurred during those prison years changed the story line of his life. On May 10, 1994, he was inaugurated as South Africa's first democratically elected president. The former prisoner became the president.

What We Miss When We Don't Forgive

One last wish.

The longing of a dying mother's heart.

A wish that only one person could have satisfied. But he didn't.

As I mentioned earlier, my childhood was a cauldron of violent arguments, alcohol-induced rage, and physically terrifying fights. My parents were a mess. Their kids were even messier.

Yes, I met Jesus in a powerful way when I was fourteen years old, and my mom soon followed. Three years later, my mean old dad accepted Christ and became one of the sweetest men I've ever known. Our family was a portrait of mercy and grace painted by the hand of an all-loving God. A lot of forgiveness took place over the next thirty years as God reshaped and remolded once-hardened hearts. But not everyone received the gift.

Some held it at arm's length and said, "No thanks. I'm hanging on to my hate." Some chose to cling to bitterness and grasp resentment with a tight, unrelenting fist. And the gift of grace was refused.

My mom did not get her final wish . . . to see her son one more time. I was sad for her, but mostly I was sad for him. He missed the blessing of seeing the miracle of mom's gentleness, mom's humble kindness, mom's overflowing love for her family. He missed the preciousness of her final days.

"The refusal to forgive is a toxic memory that endlessly pulls the painful past into the present. The toxic memory of the unforgiven past poisons the present and contaminates the future."[7]

Friend, I don't want you to miss out on a single blessing God has for you. Not a one. Nothing will block the flow of grace and hold you hostage like an unforgiving heart. You don't offer forgiveness because the offender needs it but because you need it.

Again, from Pastor Zahnd, "The world of bitterness and resentment is a very small, ever-shrinking world. It is a world of ever-diminishing possibilities. . . . Everything remains chained to the past, and the suffered injustice becomes the single informing event in the life of the embittered soul."[8]

There is a saying that time heals all wounds, but that is simply not true. In many cases, time serves as an insidious toxin that picks at scabs, infects open wounds, and digs in a little deeper with every remembrance. If you have an infected laceration on your leg, the last thing you want to do is give it more time. Left untreated, your leg could become gangrenous and need to be removed.

No, what you need to do is clean out the wound and apply medicine for it to heal.

It is the same with our hearts, minds, and emotions. When we are hurt, we must clean out the wound and apply the salve of forgiveness for it to heal.

The good news is that you never have to offer forgiveness on your own strength. Forgiveness is a concert of grace, with the Trinity including you in the music. You simply make a choice and sing along.

What We Become When We Don't Forgive

If you refuse to forgive the person or persons who have victimized, abused, or mistreated you, you are in danger of basing your entire identity on the injustice and allowing it to misshape your future and your character. The bitterness and resentment will eventually not be solely against the one who hurt you but will bleed over into other relationships as well. It will move from something that happened to you to someone you become.

Yes, the past shapes who we are, but we must not allow the pain of what has been done to us to hold us hostage. Make sure that the reasons you are the way you are do not become excuses to stay that way. Jesus died so you could live free. What a slap in His face when we say, "No thanks." It is forgiveness that breaks the chains of a bitter heart and sets us free from the prison of a painful past.

Paul warns us that a bitter heart can open a door for Satan to slide in and set up shop (2 Cor. 2:10–11; Eph. 4:31; Heb. 12:15). A bitter heart makes you a slow-moving target for the enemy.

Henry and Richard Blackaby explain it well:

> Bitterness has a tenacious way of taking root deep within the soul and resisting all efforts to weed it out. . . . Time, rather than diminishing the hurt, only seems to sharpen the pain. . . . You find yourself rehearsing the offense over and over again, each time driving the root of bitterness deeper within your soul. . . . Bitterness is easy to justify. You can get so used to a bitter heart that you are even comfortable with it, but it will destroy you. Only God is fully aware of its destructive potential.[9]

Malcolm Smith gives this analogy:

We find some perverse joy in licking old wounds. We return to the hurts again and again, reliving them in a movie we play in the theater of our minds . . . a movie in which we are the stars. We see ourselves abused, wronged—but oh so right. Every time we play this movie in our imagination we bear again what each person said or didn't say, what was done and how it was done. We cling to our memories because in our darkened minds we believe that if we forget, the one who hurt us may go free! . . . Bitterness arises from the belief that the person who hurt us owes us and must somehow pay us back.[10]

The truth is, many times the person we are holding a grudge against isn't even aware of it or doesn't care about the ill feelings. Ultimately, the only person being hurt is the person refusing to forgive. When we don't forgive, it is like we are trying to punish the person by banging our own head against the wall and saying, "Here, take that!" As I mentioned before, perhaps the person doesn't *deserve* to be forgiven. Perhaps you don't want to let the offender off the hook. None of us deserves to be forgiven, but look at how God forgave you and me. If we got what we deserved, we would all be sentenced to eternity in hell. But God gives us grace (receiving what we don't deserve) and mercy (not receiving what we do deserve).

In essence, choosing not to forgive is like picking at a scab and not allowing the wound to heal. When we offer forgiveness, we open the way for healing to take place and the wound to become a beautiful scar God can use.

How many times must we forgive? Is there any offense that warrants unforgiveness?

In Matthew 18:21–22, Peter asks Jesus, "Lord, how many times shall I forgive my brother or sister who sins against me? Up to seven times?" Jesus answers, "I tell you, not seven times, but seventy-seven times."

Sometimes I think I like Peter's idea better—seven strikes and you're out. But Jesus tells us to put no limit on forgiveness. He even gives us a story to drive the point home.

> Therefore, the kingdom of heaven is like a king who wanted to settle accounts with his servants. As he began the settlement, a man who owed him ten thousand bags of gold was brought to him. Since he was not able to pay, the master ordered that he and his wife and his children and all that he had be sold to repay the debt.
>
> At this the servant fell on his knees before him. "Be patient with me," he begged, "and I will pay everything back." The servant's master took pity on him, canceled the debt and let him go.
>
> But when that servant went out, he found one of his fellow servants who owed him a hundred silver coins. He grabbed him and began to choke him. "Pay back what you owe me!" he demanded.
>
> His fellow servant fell to his knees and begged him, "Be patient with me, and I will pay it back."
>
> But he refused. Instead, he went off and had the man thrown into prison until he could pay the debt. When the other servants saw what had happened, they were outraged and went and told their master everything that had happened.
>
> Then the master called the servant in. "You wicked servant," he said, "I canceled all that debt of yours because you begged me to. Shouldn't you have had mercy on your fellow servant just as I had on you?" In anger his master handed him over to the jailers to be tortured, until he should pay back all he owed.
>
> This is how my heavenly Father will treat each of you unless you forgive your brother or sister from your heart. (Matt. 18:23–35)

The first servant was forgiven a debt that would amount to millions of dollars by today's standards, and yet he refused to forgive a debt that would be equivalent to just a few bills. But we are to forgive as a response to being forgiven. As C. S. Lewis said, "To be a Christian means to forgive the inexcusable because God has forgiven the inexcusable in you."[11] When we read that Jesus uttered these words on the cross, "Father, forgive them," we realize we are the "them."

In Francine Rivers's novel *Leota's Garden*, she described one of her characters with these words: "She kept a list of hurts she had suffered over her lifetime. And who had caused them. She never forgot anything, never forgave. The past was like ammunition, boxed and waiting. And she was quick to load and fire."[12]

I have known women just like that. A gun loaded with words that wound—rejection laced with indifference, accusation powered by resentment, bitterness born of a need for revenge. I do not want to be that woman. I'm sure you don't either. And forgiveness is the only way to empty the ammunition and wave the flag that the war is over.

What We Gain When We Do Forgive

My friend Bonnie and I followed the GPS along winding back roads of Lancaster, Pennsylvania. I had been speaking at an event in the area and felt drawn to this place I'd come to know as Amish Grace.

Horse-drawn buggies with bearded drivers clippitty-clopped in front of us as if it were just another day. My stomach churned, wondering what we would find. Months before, a shooting had occurred in the one-room Amish schoolhouse in a small community called Nickel Mines.

Amish. School. Shooting. Never did we imagine that these words would appear together. But the unimaginable turned real on October 2, 2006, when Charles Carl Roberts IV parked his truck outside an Amish schoolhouse and carried his guns and his rage into a room of unsuspecting children.

Charles Roberts was a thirty-two-year-old dairy truck driver in Lancaster. He and his wife, Marie, along with their three young children, attended church regularly. Nine years prior to the shooting, their firstborn, a daughter, died twenty minutes after birth. But rather than let go of the pain, Charles took hold of the bitterness and held it close. Even though they subsequently had three other children, Charles clung to the anger, held on to his bitterness, and became a ticking time bomb.

In a suicide letter penned just before the shootings, Charles confessed to having sexually molested two young family members when he was twelve. The mingling of shame for his past actions with anger at God for the loss of his child created an acidic toxin that ate away at his heart and soul.

In a phone call to his wife, he left a message that said, "I'm angry at God and I need to punish some Christian girls to get even with Him."[13] In a note to his wife, Charles wrote, "I'm not worthy of you, you are the perfect wife, you deserve so much better. . . . I'm filled with so much hate towards myself, hate towards God, and an unimaginable emptiness. It seems like every time we do something fun I think about how Elise wasn't here to share it with us and I go right back to anger."[14]

Bitterness, hate, and revenge became a pit where Charles Roberts chose to live. For nine years, the need for revenge festered until his well-thought-out plan erupted into violence, death, and great loss. On a crisp fall day, Charles Roberts parked his pickup truck outside the schoolhouse, waited until the children came in from recess, and then entered armed with a .9mm handgun, a 12-gauge shotgun, a .30-06 rifle, a stun gun, and six hundred rounds of ammunition. He ordered the teacher, a handful of visiting adults, and sixteen boys to leave. Then he commanded the remaining ten girls, ages six to thirteen, to line up along the chalkboard. He shot them in the head. Five died. Five lay in critical condition. He then turned the gun on himself.

It doesn't get any worse than this for me as a mom. I can barely stand to type the words. My eyes burn. My heart hurts. But I write of this story for two reasons. One, to show the great extent to which bitterness can ruin a life when we won't let go. Two, to show the great extent to which forgiveness can heal when we do.

What happened after the shooting shocked the world. The Amish community quickly realized that Roberts's widow and children were also victims of the shooting. They had lost a husband, a father, and their privacy. They also had to bear the shame of what their family member had done to innocent children and their families. Within hours of the shooting, a group from the Amish community showed up at the Robertses' house with compassion that defied human logic. They brought condolences, food, and most importantly, they brought forgiveness. That same evening, several miles away, another Amish man from their community went to see the killer's father. He held the retired policeman in his arms and offered words of comfort and compassion.

Perhaps the most dramatic display of grace occurred at the killer's funeral when thirty-five to forty Amish crested the hill of the cemetery to mourn with the family. The funeral director recalled the moving moment: "I was lucky enough to be at the cemetery when the Amish families of the children who had been killed came to greet Marie Roberts and offer their forgiveness. And that is something I'll never forget, not ever. I knew that I was witnessing a miracle."[15]

And he was.

Forgiveness is always a miracle. It changed the story line coming out of Nickel Mines. Instead of the Nickel Mines tragedy, media outlets began to speak of the Nickel Mines miracle. The extraordinary display of forgiveness did not lessen the horror of what happened within those four walls of the schoolhouse, but grace eclipsed the story of the slaughter. As the authors of the book *Amish Grace* explained, "Journalists found themselves reporting a story that they had not set out to cover."[16]

And isn't that what the cross is all about? Jesus, an innocent man murdered on a cruel Roman cross. Jesus, who forgave His killers and rose again to forgive again and tell them so. Jesus, who forgives you and me and gives us life. The cross, a symbol of gruesome execution transformed into a symbol of mercy and grace. Amish grace changed the story line of Nickel Mines. God's forgiving grace changed the story line of Genesis chapter 3. And extending grace can change the story line of your life as well. Forgiveness allows you to break free of the hindrance of bitterness, move forward in grace, and live bold for God.

SIX

When Your Rooster Crows

Let Go of Shame-Filled Condemnation
and Take Hold of Grace-Filled Acceptance

I sat on my back porch wrapped in my fuzzy, worn robe—the one that's twenty years old but I just can't seem to get rid of. The birch tree leaves shivered in the cool morning crispness, and the gerbera daisies that had been sleeping beneath the soil through the winter months stretched their faces to the sun . . . just a bit higher than the day before. Then I heard him. The rooster.

ER-er-ER-er-ERRRR. I'm not sure where he lives, but it's within earshot.

ER-er-ER-er-ERRRR. I thought of Peter. I thought of me. I thought of you.

You know the story. At the dinner table, on the night before Jesus went to the cross, He had a chat with his friend Peter. He referred to Peter by his pre-disciple-days name—Simon.

"Simon, Simon, Satan has asked to sift all of you as wheat. But I have prayed for you, Simon, that your faith may not fail. And when you have turned back, strengthen your brothers."

But he replied, "Lord, I am ready to go with you to prison and to death."

Jesus answered, "I tell you, Peter, before the rooster crows today, you will deny three times that you know me." (Luke 22:31–34)

A few hours later, Peter did just that. Denied that he even knew Jesus. Three times. And then the rooster crowed. *ER-er-ER-er-ERRRR.*

And Peter "went outside and wept bitterly" (22:62). He cried and cried and cried.

The next morning the rooster crowed. And Peter remembered his failure.

And the next morning the rooster crowed. And Peter remembered his failure.

And the next, and the next, and the next.

With every cock-a-doodle-doo came a fresh reminder. First thing in the morning. Have you ever been there? I have. I have failed. I have cried and cried and cried. I have remembered. And even though I had asked God to forgive me, and I knew that He had, the rooster still crowed in my heart, and I remembered my failure all over again.

We all have heard the rooster crow in our own hearts at one time or another. Shame, condemnation, and regret are heavy burdens to bear, and the devil is more than willing to help you strap them on every morning . . . as faithful as a rooster's crow greets the sun.

Shame and condemnation will hold you hostage—locked away from the thriving faith God intends. Shame calls out, "Remember what you did? Remember what you said? Shame on you!" Condemnation echoes, "And you call yourself a Christian? Who are you kidding? You're a loser, a fake, a failure. That's who you really are."

And it is all lies.

The Past Does Not Define You

Yes, Moses remembered how the enslaved Hebrews had not believed him or listened to him forty years ago. Yes, he most likely held on to resentment and bitterness for the way they had treated him. But there's more to his question, "What if they don't believe me or listen to me?" I imagine as he listened to God speak through the burning bush with one ear, he heard the rooster crow in his other.

Cock-a-doodle-doo, remember what you did, how you failed, why you ran?

Moses remembered forty years earlier when he *had* tried to help these same people and they did not listen to him—did not believe him. *I've already tried to rescue those people once,* he must have thought. *I failed. I messed up. I went about it all the wrong way. Now I'm hiding out on the backside of the wilderness taking care of these smelly sheep!*

Remember, earlier, the Israelites *had not* appreciated Moses's interference, Pharaoh *had not* ignored his crime, and Moses *had not* become the hero of his people. Pharaoh put a bounty on his head, and Moses ran for his life. He failed and he bailed.

So here is God commissioning him to go back to these same people who ran him out of town forty years earlier. The same people who rejected him, belittled him, and scorned him with the words "Who made you ruler and judge over us?"

Moses didn't bring it up in his conversation with God, but I'd wager he thought about his failure every day of his miserable life.

He most likely thought:

I am such a failure.

I am such a coward.

I am so weak.

I am so stupid.

I can't do anything right.

I'll never amount to anything.

He might have tried to put his failure out of his mind, but it was always with him, just a memory away. And this is what trips us up every time. When we hang on to past foibles and failures, they stand in the way of God's calling on our lives. When we allow our past mistakes and missteps to falsely define our identity, we're held hostage by them.

If you let him, the devil will take the wrong you've done and try to convince you it is who you are. He slaps a label on you, and before you know it you're monogramming it on your shirt pocket. In her book *Unglued*, Lysa TerKeurst says this: "Those labels start out as little threads of self-dissatisfaction but ultimately weave together into a straitjacket of self-condemnation."[1] The truth is, your past is something you did; it is not who you are. Just because you failed does not mean you *are* a failure.

Like the words on your rearview mirror warn, "Objects may appear closer than they are." Looking back can often cause you to magnify your mistakes and fixate on your faults. Both can cause you to minimize your God-given abilities and calling. But the truth is, failure is never final; there is always more of the story to be written.

God uses your past to develop you but not to define you. He uses your past to help you be a better person but not to hinder you from being all He has created you to be and to do. It is often through the fiery trials of failure that success is forged. You need to learn from negative life experiences through the tutelage of the Holy Spirit but not fixate on the failure and live paralyzed by the past.

If you let Him, God will use every stinking one of your mistakes to form and fashion you into who He created you to be. And while Satan tries to use your past as a stumbling block, God uses your past as a stepping-stone on the path to living life to the full.

Your mistakes do not take God by surprise. You'll never hear Him say, "Well, I didn't see *that* coming." No, He knew what you would do and when you would do it. And His plan of forgiveness was already in place. His plan of redemption is but a confession away.

God's desire is for you to confess quickly, repent sincerely, and accept His forgiveness totally. Then take the lesson learned and move on. It is only then that you will be able to walk in the freedom He intends.

The Stumbling Block of Shame

Shame has been around since Genesis 3. Before Adam and Eve sank their teeth into the forbidden fruit, there was no shame. But as soon as they disobeyed God, the words "They were naked and ashamed" were born. And even though that was several thousand years ago, shame looks and feels the same now as it did "in the beginning."

This is what shame does to you:

- Shame hides: Adam and Eve hid from God, or at least tried to.
- Shame denies: Adam and Eve both denied they had done anything wrong.
- Shame blames: Rather than admit their failure, Adam blamed Eve, Eve blamed Satan, and Satan just smiled.
- Shame tries to cover up: Adam and Eve tried to cover up their sin with fig leaves.
- Shame causes fear: After they sinned, Adam and Eve hid from God in fear.

We face the same challenges of shame today. Are you hiding from God? Are you denying your failure rather than admitting or confessing what you've done? Are you blaming other people for your mistakes rather than taking responsibility for your own actions? Are you trying to cover up your failure with designer clothes, a well-decorated home, a high-powered job, a great haircut, a spit-shined family, a forced perma-smile? Are you afraid of what others would think about you if they knew the real you? Are you fearful of facing God? If you notice any of these characteristics of shame in your life, please know that God wants to wash it all away. He lovingly calls to you and to me just as He did to Adam and Eve: "Where are you?" (Gen. 3:9).

Guilt is not necessarily a bad thing. Someone who never feels guilty for the wrongs they've committed is known as a psychopath. Godly guilt brought on by the conviction of the Holy Spirit is meant to bring you to confession, repentance, and receiving forgiveness. The difference between shame and guilt is that guilt is because of something you did. Shame is something you believe you are. Guilt says, "What I did was horrible." Shame says, "I am horrible."

"Condemnation will construct gallows out of your flaws and failure," pastor Steven Furtick says. "But the Spirit's conviction will point you to the Cross, where the cost of those sins has already been satisfied."[2] Jesus took the punishment for our sins, and God has declared us not guilty. With His last breaths, Jesus uttered the Greek word *tetelisti*. Traditionally that word has been translated, "It is finished." But it also means, "paid in full." At the cross, all prophecies were fulfilled—all debts for sin were paid.

Conviction comes from the Holy Spirit, but accusation does not. The crushing words of accusation are destructive—always destructive. They are meant to hold you hostage in failure's vise grip. The promptings of the Spirit comb out tangled thoughts of deception and shame and bring a calm relief with confession, repentance, and forgiveness.

When Jesus died on the cross, His blood ran over the cursed thorns and onto the ground below. What a beautiful picture of Jesus's blood covering the very curse—the thorns—that were part of humankind's punishment from the Garden of Eden. Grace all around.

God buries the shame of yesterday and resurrects new beginnings and new callings. For Moses, that moment was at the burning bush. For you, it is right here, right now.

The Healing Balm of Grace

Jesus reminds us that He did not come into the world to condemn the world, but to save the world (John 12:47). Most Christians think the word *save* means deliverance from eternal punishment, separation from God, or hell. And while that is true, it also means "to heal" or "to make whole." Jesus told the woman who had been bleeding for twelve years, "Your faith has healed you. Go in peace and be freed from your suffering" (Mark 5:34). He told the woman who washed His feet with her tears and anointed His feet with oil, "Your faith has saved you; go in peace" (Luke 7:50). The Greek word translated "healed" and "saved" is from the same root word: *sōzō*. For both women, Jesus healed their bodies, saved their souls, and removed their shame. With both women, Jesus's words of *sōzō* were the chain cutters that set them free from physical, emotional, and spiritual disease to physical, emotional, and spiritual health. Their shame was removed. Their hearts were healed. Their souls were saved.

So being saved is about much more than where you will spend eternity. It is also about living fully and free in the here and now. Don't let the devil tell you anything different.

Paul wrote, "Therefore, there is now no condemnation for those who are in Christ Jesus" (Rom. 8:1). None. Nada. Zero. There's no room for shame in that. "Those who look to him are radiant; their faces are never covered with shame" (Ps. 34:5).

This is what grace does for you:

1. Grace calls you out of hiding: After Adam and Eve hid in the bushes, God called out, "Where are you?" He called them out of hiding and He's still calling us out of hiding today.
2. Grace invites confession: Grace discourages denial of wrongdoing and encourages admission of guilt. We can't change anything until we acknowledge its presence within us. *"If we*

confess our sins, He is faithful and righteous to forgive us our sins and to cleanse us from all unrighteousness" (1 John 1:9 NASB).

3. Grace offers forgiveness: Because of grace, we can be forgiven of all our failures (Eph. 1:7).

4. Grace initiates change: Because of grace, we are being transformed into His likeness with ever-increasing glory (2 Cor. 3:18).

5. Grace removes fear: "There is no fear in love [dread does not exist], but full-grown (complete, perfect) love turns fear out of doors and expels every trace of terror!" (1 John 4:18 AMPC).

Shame is a strong emotion brought on by a refusal to accept God's forgiveness. Grace is a balm to those emotions that soothes the soul, heals the heart, and sets the prisoner free. Don't let the enemy hold you hostage by accusing you of things for which God has already forgiven you.

God longs for you to be all He created you to be and to do all He's planned for you to do. But you can't if you are walking around under a cloud of shame, dragging a boatload of regret behind you.

The devil is fully aware of the power of shame to stymie your potential. That's why he tries so hard to keep you wallowing in it. As long as you allow your past failure to hold you hostage, you will never rise to the level of freedom and joy that is waiting one belief away.

"So if the Son sets you free, you will be free indeed" (John 8:36). Take hold of that truth and move forward to enjoy the adventurous life of faith God has planned for you.

The Freedom of Forgiveness

"I just can't believe I did it," Laura cried. "I had three abortions and I love children! How could I have killed my children?"

This was the rooster that crowed in Laura's heart every morning of her life. Even though she had asked God to forgive her several times, Laura had not let go of her past mistakes and forgiven herself. She put on the cloak of shame and condemnation every morning when she slipped out of bed.

Not many people know of Laura's abortions. She is a faithful Christian who hides her pain well—except with those who know her best. One day I attempted to love her to health and healing.

"Laura, you were a teenager when you had those abortions," I said. "That was thirty years ago and you weren't a Christian. You are a new creation now. The old is gone, the new has come. The old Laura is gone—she doesn't exist any longer. God forgave you the moment you asked. Your sin has been thrown as far as the east is from the west."

"I know," she replied, "but I just can't forgive myself."

For thirty years, Laura has operated under a spirit of condemnation. Every time she looks into the eyes of a child, including her own, she feels shame for what she did. And the rooster crows.

Some triggers of shame are as predictable as the rising sun. Others are a trap door that springs open by surprise.

The anniversary of an abortion.

The scent of a particular cologne.

The anniversary of a divorce.

The laughter of a child.

A movie.

A song.

A look.

Triggers engage the senses to remember the failure and the shame. But what if we allowed God to change all that? What if we allowed those triggers to become reminders of God's amazing grace that pulled us from the pit, wiped off the mud, and set our feet on the solid ground of forgiveness and freedom? What if we answered the caw of shame with the song of grace?

God forgave Laura years ago. He wiped her slate clean and wrote "forgiven" in bright red letters across the ledger of her life. God longs for Laura to operate under a spirit of grace, mercy, and forgiveness, but He cannot force her to open the present and enjoy the gift nestled within. She must receive it. She must believe it.

Receiving grace and forgiveness for the wrongs we've committed is an act of faith. "It is difficult to fathom such extravagant, unconditional love, yet so many of us leave His gift unopened. We admire its wrapping or marvel at its enormity, but avoid getting too close. Something within us cannot grasp the idea that God meant this for us, and so we put conditions on accepting His gift."[3]

No one deserves the grace and mercy of God, but for some reason, He has decided to immerse us in it. In *The Ragamuffin Gospel*, Brennan Manning explains, "To live by grace means to acknowledge my whole life story, the light side and the dark. In admitting my shadow side I learn who I am and what God's grace means. As Thomas Merton put it, 'A saint is not someone who is good but who experiences the goodness of God.'"[4]

Just as clearly as God has forgiven Laura and thrown her sins into the deepest of seas, Satan, the father of lies, reminds her of her failures and casts the line to fish them out. And as long as she is willing to take the bait, he is going to keep throwing out the line. She needs to put up a sign that says, "No fishing allowed." And so do you.

God's grace is greater than your mistakes and failures—greater than your sins. And I'm not just talking about the sins you committed before you came to Christ but also the ones you've committed since. Those are the ones the devil really likes to pull up from the deepest of seas where God has thrown them. He thrives on reminding you of the ways you continue to struggle with alcohol, gossip, lust, greed, envy, pride, and a host of other human frailties. But there is no place you can go that is so far away from God's grace that He can't redeem, restore, and renew your heart.

We all make mistakes, just different ones. A successful person is one who learns from her mistakes, gets up, and tries again. I love what Thomas Edison said after a fire destroyed his laboratory and his life's work. "Just think, all our mistakes have been burned up and we have a chance to start all over again."[5]

God's mercy and compassion are new every morning (Lam. 3:22–23), which, interestingly enough, is when that rooster crows.

Sometimes the hardest person to forgive is the woman who looks back at you in the mirror every morning. Author David Seamands said, "There is no forgiveness from God unless you freely forgive your brother from your heart. And I wonder if we have been too narrow in thinking that 'brother' only applies to someone else. What if YOU are the brother or sister who needs to be forgiven, and you need to forgive yourself?"[6]

The Hidden Key Surrendered

When I was a teenager, my high school was just a few miles from my home. Lunch break was a mere thirty-five minutes, but I enjoyed driving home and taking a respite from the hustle and bustle of the crowded hallways.

Rocky Mount, North Carolina, was a sleepy little town with a railroad track that ran down the middle of downtown, dividing it into two counties, and a Hardees fast-food restaurant on every corner reminding us that the corporate office for the chain was just down the street. When I was a child, we slept with windows open, kept doors unlocked, and rode our bicycles all over town without a hint of reservation.

But times changed in the late sixties and early seventies. We began to keep our windows closed at night, our doors locked even during the day, and kids stayed much closer to home. At our house, we kept an extra key in the mailbox just inside the doorless garage.

The only people who knew it was there were our family and the mailman.

When I went home for lunch at 12:10 every day in high school, I simply reached into the mailbox to retrieve the key, and then placed it back in the box until I came home again at 3:15.

One day I came home after school at the usual time, used the hidden key, and let myself in. Before grabbing a snack, I made a beeline to the television to turn on my favorite program. When I opened the console, I realized the TV was missing. As I looked around the house, I realized several other items were gone. I called my mom at her craft shop, and she said in a panic, "Sharon, quick! Get out of there!"

When the police came, we discovered that someone had indeed broken into our house and taken many items. And how did he get in? He used the hidden key!

Apparently, someone had been watching me. He knew I came home at 12:10 and left again at 12:45. He also knew I came home from school around 3:15. So sometime between 12:45 and 3:15, he simply took the key from the mailbox, let himself in, and helped himself to whatever he so desired. Then when he had what he wanted, the thief simply locked the door behind him and put the key back in the mailbox for "safe keeping."

Looking back on the incident, I see that is exactly what Satan does when we have shame hidden in our heart. He knows where the key is hidden, and he takes it out to steal our confidence at opportune times. He reminds us of our failures when we least expect it. As long as that key is hidden, he knows exactly where to look, and he will use it against us every chance he can.

There's only one solution. Don't hide the key. Give it to God. Allow God to apply the healing balm of grace to your skinned-up soul. Take hold of your story of redemption, and then use it for good—to encourage someone else. Referencing the devil, the book of Revelation tells us, "They overcame him by the blood of the Lamb and by the *word of their testimony*" (12:11 NIV 1984). Once you turn your hurt into hope for someone going through a struggle, the devil can't use it against you any longer.

When it comes to the shameful parts of your past, you can choose to let them define you, confine you, or refine you. But most importantly, you must leave them behind you. Stop right now and ask God if you are carrying the unnecessary burden of shame. If He reveals that you are, receive God's forgiveness and let go of the shame.

The Reminder to Forget

Paul, the writer of a majority of the New Testament, was a man who could have allowed his tainted past to stymie his ministry, but he chose to let go of the past and take hold of grace. Before Saul's name was changed to Paul, he was known as a zealous persecutor of the Christian church. Luke wrote, "Saul began to destroy the church. Going from house to house, he dragged off both men and women and put them in prison" (Acts 8:3). He was in charge of watching the coats while an angry mob stoned Stephen, the first Christian martyr. On the very day he encountered Jesus on the road to Damascus, he was traveling to the high priest for permission to arrest more Christians. You can imagine his surprise when the very One he was persecuting opened the sky and spoke his name.

After Saul's life-altering encounter with Jesus, God changed his name to Paul. However, that was not the only thing God changed—Paul became a new creation. Later he wrote, "Therefore, if anyone is in Christ, he is a new creation; the old has gone, the new has come!" (2 Cor. 5:17 NIV 1984).

Paul knew more than anyone the joy of new beginnings. He rejoiced that he was not the same man he had been before he met Jesus. As we saw in chapter 5, Paul wrote, "One thing I do, forgetting what lies behind and reaching forward to what lies ahead, I press on toward the goal for the prize of the upward call of God in Christ Jesus" (Phil. 3:13–14 NASB). He let go of the past and took hold of Christ.

I wish I could forget a few things I did in my past. Don't you? However, forgetting is not so easy. Actually, it is downright impossible to completely forget the past. The idea of forgetting was a perplexing one to me. The Bible says God forgives our sins and remembers them no more (Heb. 8:12). But how does an all-knowing God forget? To get a better picture, let's look at the opposite of forget, *to remember*.

Many events in the Bible begin with the words *God remembered*: "God remembered Noah" (Gen. 8:1), "[God] remembered Abraham" (Gen. 19:29), "God remembered Rachel" (Gen. 30:22), "God heard their groaning, and he remembered his covenant with Abraham, with Isaac and with Jacob" (Exod. 2:24). In each incident, God remembering meant that He was about to do something—to act. Therefore, if God *remembering* means He is about to act, then God *forgetting* means He is *not* going to act. He says, "For I will forgive their wickedness and will remember their sins no more" (Jer. 31:34). He forgets our sins, meaning He is *no longer* going to act upon them.

Forgetting can mean the same for us. Even though we cannot wipe the past from our minds and physiologically forget, we can choose to no longer act on the past. And more importantly, we can choose to no longer allow the past to act on us.

The truth is, we never completely forget. Honestly, I'm glad. If I forgot the pain and emotional turmoil of my past sins and failures, I would be more likely to repeat them. God removes the shame and the penalty, but memory helps us avoid going down the same path again. Learn from your mistakes under the tutelage of the Holy Spirit, and then move on.

Remembering our weakness also helps us to be more compassionate with others when they fall into seductive traps. I am much more merciful now than I was thirty years ago when my mistakes were fewer. But looking at others' mistakes through the lens of my own dark past makes them less visible to the judging eye. Jesus said these words to an angry mob concerning the woman caught in adultery: "Let any one of you who is without sin be the first to throw a stone at her" (John 8:7). It was the older Pharisees, the ones with the longer lists of failures, who first dropped the stones and walked away.

To echo the words of a very wise man, "There but for the grace of God go I."

We will all make mistakes—just different ones. We will all fail—just in different ways. Many have built their success on a solid foundation of failures. Sometimes your failures become the very springboard for your ministry in this world.

The Voices in the Stands

My son played on his high school's basketball team. At one of the games, I noticed a man on the home side of the court videoing the game. I also noticed a man on the opposing side doing the same.

"Steve, who are those men with the video cameras and why are they recording the game?" I asked my husband.

"The guy in the opposing stand is from the team we'll be playing next week," he explained. "He is recording the game to study our weaknesses so our opponents will know where to attack and defeat us. The man on our side is recording the game also looking for weaknesses, but for a different reason. He will show our team their weaknesses so they can learn from them and improve, to make them better. Same video. Different purposes."

Ah, a sudden glory moment. I don't know much about sports, but I do know a bit about how the enemy works. He records our lives and looks for our weaknesses to bring us down—to plan his attack, to defeat us.

The Bible has many names for that enemy: Satan, the great serpent, the deceiver, and the devil. But the most telling name is found in Revelation 12:10: the *accuser* who accuses believers before God day and night. Some say the devil's main role is tempting humankind to sin. But I believe what trumps even temptation is his role as the accuser who shackles us with shame and condemnation once we succumb to the temptation. He paces before God saying, "She did this and she did that." He plays and replays the video in the theater of your mind, pointing out all your faults and weaknesses to bring you down. He is *against* you.

But remember, two men were creating a video of Steven's game. Just as the accuser is against you, someone else is for you. Before Jesus went to the cross, He assured His followers that He would not leave them as orphans. He promised to send the Spirit, who would encourage, enlighten, empower, and intercede for all believers. And then Jesus gave the Spirit a name: the Advocate. "But the Advocate, the Holy Spirit, whom the Father will send in my name, will teach you all things and will remind you of everything I have said to you" (John 14:26).

An advocate is someone who is for you and acts on your behalf. Yes! He is for you! And one of the ways He is for you is to convict you of sin—of something you have done that is contrary to the ways of God. God will never reveal a weakness, a sin, or a flaw in your life just for the sake of exposing it. He always reveals a deficit because it's time to make it right—to conform you to the image of His Son. The Holy Spirit awakens your senses to an area of your life you need to change, and then He helps you do it. He shows you the video and says, "Right there. See that move? Let's work on that area and improve your game."

While the accuser points out your weakness and makes you feel you can never change, the Advocate points out your weaknesses so you *can* change. It's the same video, but seen from a different perspective. So tell me, whose voice are you going to listen to? Whose voice are you going to believe?

Rooster Makes a Fine Meal

Peter made a lot of mistakes during his time with Jesus, but he made his greatest mistakes when it mattered most. He was a convoluted mix of headstrong brashness and fleet-footed cowardice. When the soldiers showed up at the Garden of Gethsemane, Peter stepped up and lopped off Marcus's ear. But when those same soldiers arrested Jesus and led Him away in chains, Peter ran for his life.

A few hours later, at Jesus's mock trial before Pilate, Peter "followed at a distance" (Luke 22:54). That's what shame will do to all of us if we allow it to hold us in its vise grip. We may still follow Jesus, but it will be at a distance. We might go to church, sing the songs, and even raise our hands a time or two, but if we carry the unnecessary—and I daresay, unbiblical—shame in our hearts, we will follow at a distance.

As I mentioned at the beginning of this chapter, a few hours after Jesus's arrest, after a trio of denials, the rooster crowed. What did Jesus have to say about Peter's failure? Three strikes, you're out? Hardly. Grace sat by the fire and looked Peter in the eye. Here's what happened.

After Jesus's resurrection, Peter had gone back to the familiar—doing what he had always done. Failure in your faith will do that to you if you're not careful. But Peter was about to learn that failure was never meant to take us back or hold us back but rather to move us forward in our faith.

Peter gathered a few of his buddies, launched the boat, and went fishing on the Sea of Galilee. After a night of nothing but empty nets, as the sun rose over the horizon, a man called from the shore, "Have you caught any fish?"

"No," Peter answered. "Not a one."

"Throw your net on the right side of the boat and you will find some," the man called out. When they did, they were unable to haul the net in because of the large number of fish.

At that moment, Peter realized it was Jesus. He jumped into the water and swam to the shore, where Jesus already had a fire burning. After breakfast, Jesus pulled Peter aside.

"Simon son of John, do you love me more than these?"

"Yes, Lord," he said, "you know that I love you."

Jesus said, "Feed my lambs."

Again Jesus said, "Simon son of John, do you love me?"

He answered, "Yes, Lord, you know that I love you."

Jesus said, "Take care of my sheep."

The third time he said to him, "Simon son of John, do you love me?" . . .

"Lord, you know all things; you know that I love you."

Jesus said, "Feed my sheep." (John 21:15–17)

Jesus removed the shroud of shame hanging from Peter's guilt-weary shoulders and rallied him to get back to the ministry to which he was called—being a fisher of men, not a fisher of fish.

Oh, friend, Peter's failure was not final, and neither is yours. It is simply one of the many stepping-stones God uses to get you where you need to be. I think of Jesus's words to Peter in that upper room: "And when you have turned back, strengthen your brothers" (Luke 22:32).

And when you have turned back . . . remember, you are not finished. Get back to doing what God has called you to do. Let go. Move forward. Live bold.

God's forgiveness is always complete, total, and comprehensive. "If we [freely] admit that we have sinned and confess our sins, He is faithful and just (true to His own nature and promises) and will forgive our sins [dismiss our lawlessness] and [continuously] cleanse us from all unrighteousness [everything not in conformity to His will in purpose, thought, and action]" (1 John 1:9 AMPC).

However, the accuser continues to crow—reminding us of our past sins and failures. He tries to drown out the song of grace with the caw of shame. He crows. We remember. Perhaps even weep with Peter behind the wall.

You know what I've decided? Rooster makes a fine meal. Let's wring the rooster's neck and cook him up once and for all. Don't allow the enemy to accuse you of what God has already forgiven you for. Don't let him fool you into thinking the cross wasn't enough.

Let go of shame and take hold of grace.

I wonder what went through Peter's mind the next time he heard the rooster crow. I think he smiled and thought of God's amazing grace. That's what I'm going to do tomorrow when I hear that rooster crow in my heart. I hope you do too.

seven

Give Fear the Boot

Let Go of Weak-Kneed Worry
and Take Hold of Sure-Footed Confidence

Moses reached back forty years for his objection: "What if they don't believe me or listen to me?" But the words *what if* also pointed a shaky finger to the future failure he feared would come. Memory tightened its fingers around his throat and squeezed. Fear of going back to Egypt rose like gall.

Yes, he remembered how he had failed and bailed. Yes, he remembered how the Israelites had shunned and shamed him. Yes, he remembered how the Egyptians had disdained and dishonored him. All that was wrapped up in the two little words *what if*. But even more than being held hostage by the past, he was afraid of moving from the safety of his little Medianite cul-de-sac and into the destiny God had planned for him all along.

Fear can hold you hostage and cause you to forfeit God's promises. Anxious thoughts shrink your view of God, while trusting Him keeps the lens rightly focused. When you're too timid to trust God, fear hems you in and keeps life small. Faith grabs fear by the nape of the neck and gives you the courage to move forward and live bold.

The apostle John wrote, "There is no fear in love. But perfect love drives out fear, because fear has to do with punishment. The one who fears is not made perfect in love" (1 John 4:18). Another translation says it this way: "There is no fear in love [dread does not exist], but full-grown (complete, perfect) love turns fear out of doors and expels every trace of terror! For fear brings with it the thought of punishment, and [so] he who is afraid has not reached the full maturity of love [is not yet grown into love's complete perfection]" (AMPC).

I love that! "Love turns fear out of doors and expels every trace of terror!" Perfect love, God's love, gives fear the boot. Fear stands at the doorway of our destinies and dares us to step inside. It bullies us into believing that if we step across the threshold we will fail, or worse yet, God will fail us. Fear holds a "Danger! Keep Out!" sign over our preordained adventures and pokes drain holes in our Spirit-filled confidence.

What if . . .

Oswald Chambers once said, "The remarkable thing about fearing God is that when you fear God you fear nothing else, whereas if you do not fear God you fear everything else."[1]

The fear of rejection and the unknown can be paralyzing. It is an insidious force that has stymied the dreams and sabotaged God's promises for many of God's children. That's what Moses had to overcome. That's what you and I must overcome if we are going to move forward and live bold.

Truth Overrules Fear

Several years ago, the movie *The Patriot* was filmed near my hometown. It was a movie about the Revolutionary War, and several of my neighbors auditioned to become extras for the film. My neighbor Mike was one of them. He had lost a leg due to cancer when he was in his twenties and wore a prosthetic limb from the knee down. "Surely they'll pick me," he said with a quick wit. "I've already got a fake leg! I'll be perfect for the war scenes."

They did not pick Mike for the battle scenes. But they did choose his nine-year-old son, Michael, to be the stand-in for Benjamin Martin's (Mel Gibson's) young son, Samuel. For months, Michael wore his hair long with extensions, slipped on Italian knickers and knee-high stockings, and acted the part of a colonial American boy. He traveled to rural South Carolina where part of the movie was filmed and received an education in the production of the silver screen. Michael saw how producers and makeup artists made something appear real when it wasn't.

The movie was a bloody reenactment of the horrors of the Revolutionary War, which I would have normally shied away from. But we were eager to see Michael's acting debut. I had to cover my eyes during several of the gruesome guts-and-gore war scenes. However, little Michael didn't even bat an eye. Why? He knew it wasn't real.

During one scene, Mel Gibson pummeled a British soldier and landed a hatchet square in the middle of his bloody forehead. Once again, I quickly covered my eyes. Michael watched unfazed. His comment?

"That's not real. That guy walked around with that hatchet in his head for three days. We even ate lunch together and he had that hatchet with fake blood glued to his head the whole time. It isn't real."

Michael knew what was real and what wasn't real, and that removed all fear. Oh, that we could do the same. Anxiety, worry, and fear wrap you up in yourself, trapping your own thoughts in a suffocating stranglehold. When you know the truth of God's love—rather, when you actually believe the truth of God's love—it removes the paralyzing fear that holds you hostage. The truth not only sets you free but also becomes the wind beneath your sails to take you on the exciting adventures God has planned.

Action Breeds Confidence

Some respond to fear by retreating to the safety of cul-de-sac Christianity, which is actually one of the most dangerous places of all. Dale Carnegie once said, "Inaction breeds doubt and fear. Action breeds confidence and courage. If you want to conquer fear, do not sit home and think about it. Go out and get busy."[2]

You will not become more courageous and learn to live bold by avoiding your fears. Courage based on the faithfulness and love of God is strengthened with every step of faith, no matter how small. Write the letter. Start the conversation. Sign up to volunteer. Create the blog. Make the donation. Mend the relationship. Each step of obedience creates momentum that helps you break through the stronghold of fear.

The woman who lives life to the fullest is generally the one who is willing to do and to dare. Allow God to infuse you with an enthusiasm and gusto that gives fear the boot right out the door, with you following close behind.

As you consider what might happen if you step out in faith, you must also consider what will happen if you play it safe and don't. When we live bold, we will experience God's blessings. When we don't, we won't.

The fact is, we all experience fear at one time or another. We fear things we can't control, and fear things we can. We fear terrorist attacks and breast cancer. We fear losing a child and the death of a spouse. We fear financial loss and relational ruin. We fear being alone and being lonely.

Some researchers say over 366 verses in the Bible encourage us not to be afraid. I'm not sure if that number is correct, but I do know "Fear not" is a continuous thread weaving a tapestry of truth throughout the Scriptures. Why is that? God knew we would struggle with it!

"Have I not commanded you? Be strong and courageous," God encouraged Joshua. "Do not be afraid; do not be discouraged, for the LORD your God will be with you wherever you go" (Josh. 1:9).

God encouraged the Israelites:

> Do not fear, for I have redeemed you;
> I have summoned you by name; you are mine.
> When you pass through the waters,
> I will be with you;
> and when you pass through the rivers,
> they will not sweep over you.
> When you walk through the fire,
> you will not be burned;
> the flames will not set you ablaze.
> For I am the LORD your God,
> the Holy One of Israel, your Savior.
>
> Isaiah 43:1–3

The Psalms are a storehouse of verses encouraging us to respond to all of life's situations and difficulties through bold believing, tenacious trust, and courageous faith—verses that embolden believers to take action despite the trembling knees. One example is Psalm 56. David had been seized by the Philistines in Gath and started to feel afraid. But rather than give in to his unsettling fear, he changed his focus to his unchanging God.

> When I am afraid, I put my trust in you.
> In God, whose word I praise—
> in God I trust and am not afraid.
> What can mere mortals do to me?
>
> Psalm 56:3–4

Notice David did not ignore his fear. Rather, he spoke to his fear, and the truth of God's faithfulness shooed it away. We can follow David's example and profess with him, "When I am afraid of _____, I put my trust in You."

Your fear is fueled by your focus. Your faith is fueled by your focus. What are you focusing on today? What thoughts are fueling your tank?

I don't want to die with gas still in the tank. I want to live bold—for God to use me until I'm all used up. But to do that, I must put the fear of failure, embarrassment, humiliation, or intimidation aside and take a step of faith.

Choices Determine Destinies

One day Jesus told a parable to a group of listeners. We've come to know it as the parable of the talents, but it is really more the parable of the three choices. Jesus was explaining what the kingdom of heaven would be like in common terms.

> For it is just like a man about to go on a journey, who called his own slaves and entrusted his possessions to them. To one he gave five talents, to another, two, and to another, one, each according to his own ability; and he went on his journey. Immediately the one who had received the five talents went and traded with them, and gained five more talents. In the same manner the one who had received the two talents gained two more. But he who received the one talent went away, and dug a hole in the ground and hid his master's money.
>
> Now after a long time the master of those slaves came and settled accounts with them. The one who had received the five talents came up and brought five more talents, saying, "Master, you entrusted five talents to me. See, I have gained five more talents." His master said to him, "Well done, good and faithful slave. You were faithful with a few things, I will put you in charge of many things; enter into the joy of your master."

Also the one who had received the two talents came up and said, "Master, you entrusted two talents to me. See, I have gained two more talents." His master said to him, "Well done, good and faithful slave. You were faithful with a few things, I will put you in charge of many things; enter into the joy of your master."

And the one also who had received the one talent came up and said, "Master, I knew you to be a hard man, reaping where you did not sow and gathering where you scattered no seed. And I was afraid, and went away and hid your talent in the ground. See, you have what is yours."

But his master answered and said to him, "You wicked, lazy slave, you knew that I reap where I did not sow and gather where I scattered no seed. Then you ought to have put my money in the bank, and on my arrival I would have received my money back with interest. Therefore take away the talent from him, and give it to the one who has the ten talents." (Matt. 25:14–28 NASB)

This story gives me chills every time I read it. For you see, God has given each and every one of us gifts—gifts He has purposed for us to use, invest, and multiply. And I'm not just talking about money, but gifts in our inner being. He has given you talents and abilities He expects you to use to further the kingdom and minister to others.

So what kept the servant with one talent from doing so? Fear. Giving in to fear prevented him from investing what he had. I think the master would have been more pleased if the servant had said, "Lord, I invested the talent and unfortunately lost it all." At least he would have tried. At least he would have made some effort. But the master saw him as evil and lazy.

Fear makes us lazy. Think about that a minute. A fearful person does little.

Moving forward despite the fear gets the spiritual couch potato out from under the afghan and into the life she was meant to live.

Perhaps you're thinking God hasn't given you much to work with. Maybe you think you're only a one-talent girl. He did, after all, entrust the servants with talents "according to their ability." You look at what other folks are doing for God with their five talents and think yours don't really matter much anyway. Nothing could be farther from the truth.

It could be that the servant with the five talents started out with one talent a few years back. The master saw what he did with that one—how he turned it into two. Then when he went on his next trip, the master gave that servant two talents, which he turned into four. So on this particular journey, the master entrusted this servant with five!

If we don't use what God has given us because of fear, then He will not entrust us with more. It could very well be that He will take away what He's given us and give it to someone else who has the courage to use her gifts and talents to accomplish her God-given purpose.

There's always a bit of fear when it comes to taking a step of faith, but step we must! Don't let the fear win. It's not worth it.

I always thought a talent was just a few pieces of silver or gold. Boy, was I wrong. In biblical days, a talent referred to the largest unit of currency at the time. It was the heaviest or largest biblical unit of measurement for weight, equal to about seventy-five pounds or thirty-five kilograms.[3] The one who possessed five talents of gold or silver was a multimillionaire by today's standards. Some calculate a talent to be equivalent to twenty years' wages for the common worker.[4]

So even though the one servant received only one talent (or bag of gold), it was still no paltry amount. And again, I'm not turning this into a teaching about money. I don't think that was what Jesus was doing either. He was teaching us about being good stewards of what God has entrusted to us in every area of life.

God will never call you to do anything He will not empower and equip you to do. How sad when we hide what He has entrusted to us because of fear. If you have your talent hidden in the ground, dig it up. Once the landowner in the parable came home, it was too late for that servant with the one talent, but it is not too late for you.

I'm glad the biblical term for what Jesus was teaching about is *talents*. The NIV translates it as "bags of gold." But when I see the word *talents*, I can better associate it with God-given gifts and abilities. You have been given talents! Even if you think you have been given only one talent, you have been given one.

Don't let fear keep you from using what you have. Invest what God has given you in other people and watch your investment multiply right before your eyes. Then when your day comes, God will say, "Well done, good and faithful servant. Enter into the joy of your master."

The Song That Rocked the World

Darlene was a young mom with money worries and the stress of raising a young family. One day, when she was feeling particularly discouraged, she slipped into a room that housed her two daughters' toys and her piano. Drawing on the comforting words of the Psalms, she began putting the truths of Scripture to song. On her out-of-tune piano, she began playing until her heart lifted. She chose words that encouraged her to hold on to her faith despite any discouragement she felt. "I wrote it when I was feeling discouraged," she said. "I felt I could either scream and pull my hair out, or praise God."

Over the next few days, the song stayed with her. Two lines in the song were truths she took hold of when her circumstances seemed so dismal: "Mountains bow down and the seas will roar at the sound of your name. . . . Nothing compares to the promise I have in you." It occurred to her that the song could possibly be turned into a worship song for her church. Even though she was afraid, she gathered up enough courage to approach her worship pastor with the idea.

Darlene said, "I was terribly shy and felt a little embarrassed when I mentioned to the music pastors that I thought I had written a song. My hands were sweaty. I could hardly play it, I was so nervous. I kept starting and stopping. It took me twenty minutes to play it because I kept apologizing, 'I'm sorry. Change anything you want. I know it's probably stupid.' Eventually I made them stand with their backs to me while I played them the song. Even when they turned around and said that it was magnificent, I thought they were just being polite."[5]

A few weeks later, Darlene and the music team introduced "Shout to the Lord" at one of their worship services at Hillsong Church. Soon it began to spread from church to church. Before she even recorded it, she began receiving thank-you letters from people all over the world. "Shout to the Lord" has been sung before the pope at the Vatican, for the US president in the White House, and in churches all around the globe. And all because a young mom in Australia chose to let go of her fear, take hold of her faith, and live bold. I'm so glad she did.

Courage is not the absence of fear; it is moving forward despite the fear. Here's a secret: every time I write a book or stand up to speak, there is an element of fear. Fear of failure. Fear I won't be effective. Fear I'll forget what I was going to say. Fear the book will flop. Fear I won't be able to meet my deadline. Fear the words won't come.

But I have decided to press through the fear and move forward in faith. If you are waiting to feel unafraid before moving forward, you most likely never will. Being brave and living bold does not mean you won't be afraid. It means you move forward in faith even though you still are. It means you kick fear out the door with courage and walk past it, out into this big, wonderful world.

Worry Wastes Life

Not all fear is bad. It is good to be afraid of sticking your hand into a fire, crossing a busy street with your eyes closed, or jumping off a cliff. That is good, healthy fear. The fear I'm talking about here is fear of present circumstances and future events that may or may not happen. Being too afraid to step out and do what God has called you to do. Being so worried about the consequences that you throw trusting God out the window.

The Holy Spirit will warn you with a healthy sense of fear to protect you, but He will never stir up worry to stymie your faith. I've often heard it said that worry is a down payment on a problem you may never have. And it's true! Rehearsing your troubles before they even happen causes you to experience them many times, whereas you were meant to experience them only once—when or if they actually occur.

Most of the big challenges you will face will be the result of things you never even thought to worry about or that never even crossed your mind. They will blindside you on a Thursday afternoon at 2:00, when you never saw it coming. You will not even have known that you should have worried about the possibility.

We waste valuable time and forfeit a thriving faith when we allow "what ifs" to hold us captive.

What if I'm embarrassed?

What if I'm rejected?

What if I fall flat on my face?

What if I fail?

What if one or all of these things do happen when I step forward in obedience? I'll live. God will be right there with me.

Here's the bigger question: What if I don't step forward in obedience? What if I ignore God's prompting? I might miss out on one of His greatest blessings in my life.

Do you believe God loves you? I'm thinking you just answered yes. Then why do you worry that He doesn't have your best interest in mind? He will not allow or initiate any circumstance in your life that is not filtered through His sovereign love for you. You will make it! Life might not unfold as you imagined, but when you place your hand in His and trust in His love, you will survive and most likely thrive.

Paul had an incredible attitude about the "what ifs" in his life. He had the mind-set of *bring it on*. The Pharisees couldn't stand him, but they found his attitude made it impossible to stop him. They threw him into prison and he said, "That's okay. Give me some parchment and ink. I'll write some letters to the churches. I'll write to them about how to have joy in all circumstances."

They chained him to a prison guard and he said, "That's okay. I'll tell him about Jesus. As a matter of fact, I'll bring his whole family to Christ!"

They threatened to kill him and he said, "That's okay. I'll get to go to heaven and be with Jesus. What could be better?"

Paul faced his fears and booted them out the door with the love of God. What do you do to a guy like that?

Paul wrote, "For to me, to live is Christ and to die is gain. If I am to go on living in the body, this will mean fruitful labor for me. Yet what shall I choose? I do not know!" (Phil. 1:21–22). He wasn't worried or concerned about his future. Paul was at peace with whatever happened on his faith journey because he trusted in the character and love of God. And with a faith like that, the natural consequence is to live bold.

Turn Fear Out of Doors

The fear of "what if" doesn't evaporate if we close our eyes and wait long enough. It must be evicted, expelled, thrown out, put out, cast out, and turned out of doors—given the boot.

Listening to God's voice of truth above all others is the only way to silence the fears that rise up against you and rattle about in your head. Allowing fear to mess with your mind and rule your heart will smother your confidence and courage with an avalanche of doubt. Faith despite the fear is a deliberate confidence in the character and the love of God, whose ways you may not understand.

You either show fear the door, or it will bolt the lock to keep you out of the places God has prepared for you to go and stop you from doing all He has planned for you to do. Fear has no choice but to leave the premises when you stand on the promises of God and say, "You are not welcome here."

Fear of "what if" stands at the doorway of our destinies, daring us to step inside. And if we give in to fear and ignore God's plan, He will pick someone else. Then we're left wondering why God doesn't work in our life like He does in other people's lives.

What If Your Worst "What If" Does Happen?

Some people just seem happy and positive all the time. They appear to never worry and fret. These people act like they eat rainbows for breakfast and ride a unicorn to work. But life isn't all lucky charms. Sometimes it is just plain hard. We anticipate trials. Jesus promised trouble. "In this world you will have trouble," He warned (John 16:33).

So what if the worst thing you can imagine does happen? What then?

What if my child gets sick?

What if my husband does leave?

What if I lose my job?

What if I get on a plane to go to a speaking engagement and the plane crashes?

I decided a long time ago, when I get on a plane, I'm either going to get where I'm headed or I'm going to heaven. Either one is fine with me. I know that whatever may happen in this life, God's still on His throne and He's in control.

Yes, worry is a down payment on a problem that you may never have, but sometimes you *do* have the problem. Sometimes the sinkhole is worse than you ever imagined. But here's what you can always take hold of when you feel you're being sucked down: God will be right smack-dab in the middle of your sinkhole even if your worst "what if" does occur.

What is your greatest fear? What worries threaten to hold you hostage? Perhaps you've already experienced your greatest fear. Maybe you have lost a child, gone through a divorce, foreclosed on your home. Perhaps you've already gone through radiation, filed for bankruptcy, or lost your job. If you have already experienced your greatest fears, then oddly enough, you have an advantage over those who haven't. You've seen that God does give you the strength to get through your most horrendous seasons imaginable. You've come out on the other side and realized that by the grace of God you've made it.

None of us would choose to experience the horrific losses or painful situations that are part of living on this side of heaven. But some treasures can only be discovered in dark places. One such treasure unearthed by those on the other side of their worst "what ifs" is the knowledge of God's sustaining power that got them through and held them up—that gave them the power to move on despite the losses and live bold despite the pain. That's what Gail discovered.

Aaron was Gail's only son, the older brother to two adoring sisters. Growing up an athletic middle child with two sisters herself, Gail had always wanted a son. From the moment Aaron made his first cry, he and his mom had a special bond. When he went away to college 570 miles from home, part of Gail's heart went with him. Her greatest fear was that something would happen to one of her three children.

On Christmas break during his sophomore year, Aaron and his mom were laughing and joking around in the kitchen. Then he sprang it on her. "Mom, a bunch of friends and I want to go to New York City for New Year's Eve. Would that be okay?"

"Son," she said, "bad things happen to good people on New Year's Eve in New York City!"

Then Aaron grew serious. "Mom, look at me. If anything ever happens to me, I will go to heaven. I'll be fine."

"Son, if something happened to you, and you went to heaven, you might as well take me with you. I wouldn't be able to live after that."

A few months later, Aaron called her from his cell phone. "Mom, you've got to hear this song!" Gail listened to the words from his radio, lyrics from "Who Am I" by Casting Crowns that had moved her son to call: "Who am I that the Lord of all the earth would care to know my name, would care to feel my hurt? . . . I am a flower quickly fading, here today and gone tomorrow."[6]

"That is awesome, Aaron," she replied. "Thanks for sharing it with me." She continued her work and thanked God for a son who loved her enough to spontaneously call and share something that moved him spiritually.

One hot summer day in June, Aaron's friend Tyler invited him to go rafting down the James River in their college town of Lynchburg, Virginia. The James was swollen due to heavy rains, and it promised to be an exhilarating ride. They each had their own small raft but vowed to stay close together. Tyler held on tight as he maneuvered the rapids and made it to calm waters. Then he stopped to watch Aaron do the same. Aaron also held on tight, but his raft flipped over. Aaron went under. Tyler waited for Aaron to resurface from the angry waters, but he never did.

The next four days were every parent's nightmare. Gail and several family members drove from Rhode Island to Lynchburg.

She clung to Aaron's picture and kept repeating the words of Psalm 91: "'Because he loves me,' says the LORD, 'I will rescue him; I will protect him, for he acknowledges my name'" (v. 14).

When they arrived at the river, search dogs, rescue workers, helicopters, police, and a CSI team surrounded them. But even with the hectic scramblings of the uniformed officers, Gail sensed an indescribable and undeniable peace.

The dogs picked up Aaron's scent along the bank, but there was no sign of her son. After four days, the rescue workers made the tough decision to call off the search. "We may never find his body," one said. "He may have been swept out to the bay."

"But this is my baby!" Gail cried. "You've got to find him!"

She thought of the words from Aaron's devotion book that still lay open on his nightstand—open to June 30—the day of the accident, paraphrasing Psalm 40:2: "I will pull you out of the muck and mire."

On the way back to Aaron's apartment the next morning, Vince Gill's song "Go Rest High on That Mountain" played on the radio. "Son, your work on earth is done," he sang. Stunned, Gail looked at the clock. It read 11:30.

Moments later a rescue worker called and asked Gail and her family to meet them at the fire station. When the ambulance turned the corner and came into view, she knew.

One of the men knelt down in front of Gail. "Gail," he began with tears in his eyes and a comforting soft smile on his face, "we found your boy."

"Can I see him?" she asked.

"No, Gail, you can't."

"What time did you find him," she asked with trembling lips.

"11:30 a.m.," he replied.

Before the funeral, Gail found a school paper Aaron had just written:

I am very lucky. I have never experienced the death of someone really close to me. I do have a couple of family members right now who are in bad health, so I am beginning to realize that it will be a reality for me soon. The thing that makes it worse is that I know for a fact that these family members are not saved. As for me, it is not the thought of death that scares me because I know where I will be going. . . . I hope and pray that my unsaved family comes to know Jesus as their Savior.

Gail's brother-in-law read that paper at Aaron's funeral and watched as Aaron's prayers were answered. Many people came to Christ that day, including several family members.

When I met Gail, I was struck by her breathtaking beauty, both inside and out. Blue eyes sparkle. A wide smile shines. Joy oozes. That's the best way I know to describe it. She just oozes joy, and you want to get close enough for some of it to spill over onto you. But then she told me her story. My mind wrestled, trying to reconcile the peace I saw on her face and the worst "what if" imaginable being her reality. She told me story after story of how God sustained her and her family through the next months and years—stories about how God showed up, held her up, and kept her up.

"Yes, I grieved," she said. "I still do. Even though I saw God's fingerprints throughout the entire ordeal, even though I sensed His presence surrounding our family and friends, I was still mad at Him. But God stayed right there with me. He didn't give up on me but lovingly wooed me, pursued me, and loved me back to life. He pulled *me* from the muck and mire. I knew I had to let go and take hold of the promises of God as never before. What gets me through is the knowledge that I will see Aaron again. As he reminded me before he died, we are but a flower quickly fading, here today and gone tomorrow, a vapor in the wind. Before I know it, we'll be together again."

Today Gail speaks at women's events and encourages others who have experienced great loss that there is hope in Jesus Christ. She is not afraid of what the future holds. She is looking forward to it.

Friend, whatever you are going through or will go through, know this: God will get you through, and there is still more of the abundant life to behold. He can turn even your worst "what ifs" into a portrait of beauty and grace that will amaze the world.

The Worst "What If" Imaginable

I am writing this chapter the week before Easter. More specifically, it's Friday—the day we remember Christ's crucifixion. The truth is, the worst "what if" that could ever occur already has—what if someone killed the Son of God? What if they forced a crown of piercing thorns on His head, thrashed a flesh-tearing whip embedded with sharp objects across His back, spat in His face, beat Him with fists, nailed His feet and hands to a splintery cross? What if they plunged a sword into His side? What if they murdered Jesus? What if that happened?

Oh, friend, it is with tears in my eyes that I attempt to type these words. Perhaps it is the gravity of the day I'm remembering. Perhaps it is the horror of that Friday. Perhaps.

But there's more. You know the rest. Death was not the end of the story. It never is. Three days later, God rolled the stone away from the mouth of the cave where Jesus was buried, and Hope walked out in newness of life—resurrection life.

Because of the death, resurrection, and ascension of Jesus Christ, because of the power of the Holy Spirit who now lives within us, we no longer have to buckle under the spirit of fear or go weak-kneed due to worry. We can live bold, knowing that God empowers and equips us to do everything He has called us to do.

We can refuse to bury our dreams in shallow graves of fear and live in bold obedience, expecting the best.

Jump In

I was sitting on the balcony of a condominium at the beach with my computer in my lap. In the background, I heard the excited squeals and splashes as children played in the swimming pool below.

One particular little girl caught my attention. She appeared to be about six years old and wore bright yellow water wings wrapped around her arms like blood pressure cuffs. As she stood on the side of the pool nervously flapping her arms, her daddy was poised in waist-deep water with his arms outstretched.

"Come on, honey, you can do it," he coached. "Go ahead and jump. I'm right here."

"But I'm scared," she said, whining and flapping. "You might not catch me."

"Don't be afraid. I'm right here."

"But you might move!"

"I'm not going to move. I'm not going to let anything happen to you," he assured her.

This bantering went on for at least fifteen minutes. I was amazed at the father's patience and persistence. But finally, she jumped! Applause went up all around the pool! By the end of the morning, the little girl was swimming like a minnow and making her way across the once seemingly treacherous waters.

Then God began to speak to my heart. *Sharon, sometimes you're that little girl.* And suddenly I began to see myself standing on the edge of that pool with my heavenly Father beckoning me to jump.

Come on, honey, you can do it, He coaxes. *Go ahead and jump. I'm right here.*

"But I'm scared," I cry. "You might not catch me."

Don't be afraid. I'm right here.

"But You might move!"

I'm not going to move. I'm not going to let anything happen to you, He assures me.

So here's what I've decided to do. When God calls me to dare greatly, I'm going to jump in with both feet but never let go of His hand. I hope you will too.

eight

The Measuring Stick Will Get You Stuck

Let Go of Comparison to Others and
Take Hold of Your God-Fashioned Uniqueness

After Moses's third objection, God did several miracles to prove He could do what He said He would do. He turned Moses's shepherding staff into a slithering snake and back into a staff again. He mysteriously covered Moses's hand with leprosy and miraculously made it clean again. But seeing is not necessarily believing. You can witness God do all kinds of miracles and still not believe He will do them *for you* or *through you*. Moses didn't. He had one more objection. Let's go back to the bush.

> Moses said to the LORD, "Pardon your servant, Lord. I have never been eloquent, neither in the past nor since you have spoken to your servant. I am slow of speech and tongue."
> The LORD said to him, "Who gave human beings their mouths? Who makes them deaf or mute? Who gives them sight or makes

them blind? Is it not I, the LORD? Now go; I will help you speak and will teach you what to say." (Exod. 4:10–12)

Moses was just plain old groveling at this point. I love how Eugene Peterson paraphrases his plea in *The Message*: "Master, please, I don't talk well. I've never been good with words, neither before nor after you spoke to me. I stutter and stammer" (v. 10).

Moses tried one last time to convince God he was a loser—to twist God's arm to pick someone else for the job. God didn't buy it.

I understand Moses's reservations. As I mentioned earlier, when God began to nudge me in the direction of speaking and writing, when He flung the door wide open and beckoned me to step across the threshold of my fears, I said the same thing. "I've never been good with words. Lord, do you remember the spelling train, for goodness' sake?"

See, when I was six years old, I skipped off to first grade with a new box of crayons, a crisp green dress with Swiss polka dot sleeves, and a fresh hope that I would be good enough—that someone would at least like me. But first grade only confirmed my fears. I wasn't good enough after all.

From the time my teacher held up the first spelling flash card, I knew I was in trouble. Back in the day, kindergarten focused on coloring, playing, and napping. But first grade was a whole new ball game with letters, numbers, and words. First grade had flash cards.

Remembering one exercise makes my palms clammy even today. We lined our miniature wooden chairs up in a row like a train. The conductor, Mrs. Morgan, held up a spelling flash card for the lead passenger to identify. If he or she could not correctly decipher the word on the card, that passenger lost the lead seat and had to go sit in the caboose. I spent most of the first grade in the caboose. I could not spell to save my life.

Mrs. Morgan decided she was going to give me a little extra help. After all, she had taught my brother five years earlier, and he was pretty smart. Maybe there was hope for me.

She kept me after school to work on my reading with another little boy named Mike. I might not have been very bright, but I was smart enough to figure out what being singled out with Mike meant.

For some reason I had particular trouble with the word *the*. In an effort to help me remember that all-important word, Mrs. Morgan made a name tag that read "t-h-e" and pinned it to my little chest. I had to wear this scarlet letter for two weeks. My peers taunted me with words of their own. "Why are you wearing that name tag?" "Is your name 'The'?" "Are you stupid?" "What's wrong with you?"

After two weeks, I learned how to spell the word *the*, but that's not all I learned. I learned I was stupid, not as smart as everybody else, and once again, not enough.

And now God was nudging me to write? With words? Words I had to spell? One of my greatest weaknesses? One of my insidious sources of insecurity? The very thing that put the rubber stamp on my greatest fears so long ago?

The truth is, I was not stupid. I just couldn't spell very well. Still can't. And even though I graduated from high school with honors, did well in college, and have written a passel of books, many times I've felt like that little girl sitting in the spelling train caboose.

Isn't it mind-boggling that God will sometimes take our greatest weaknesses and turn them into our greatest strengths? But that won't happen until we let go of the fear of moving forward and take hold of the hand of God with a grip of trust. We can choose to stay stuck in the caboose or come up front with the Chief Engineer.

I'm still not a good speller. However, I am not going to allow my weakness to stand in the way of my God-given purpose. I hope you won't either.

God said to Moses, God said to me, and God is saying to you, "I will teach you what to say. I will show you what to do." What more could a person ask for? What more do you and I need?

Then God invented spell check! Hallelujah.

But as you know, even spell check doesn't catch everything. One day I wrote a blog about Elijah and the widow of Zarephath recorded in 1 Kings 17. I told about how Elijah approached a destitute widow who was picking up sticks to prepare her last meal. I wrote about how the prophet asked her to make him a little cake of bread before she made one for herself and attached a promise along with it (v. 14): "[Your] jar of flour will not be used up and the jug of oil will not run dry until the day the LORD sends rain on the land," which is exactly what happened. In summary, I wrote, "Elijah kept the widow's pantry mysteriously stocked." Well, that's what I meant to say. However, I left the r out of the word *pantry*. Yep. Thousands of readers all around the world found this in their inbox: "Elijah kept the widow's *panty* mysteriously stocked."

Keeping it real here. Thought you might enjoy a good chuckle.

When I woke the following morning after my late-night post, I was greeted with a legion of commenters' responses. Glory be! "Lord, this one's on You," I moaned. "You didn't catch it. I'm just being obedient to the best of my ability."

Honestly, I think there were lots of women who needed a good laugh that day. I think God laughed too.

Okay, I've digressed, and if that little section made it through the editor's cut, it will be a miracle!

Comparison Kills Confidence

Moses hadn't always been so insecure. Look what Stephen said to the Sanhedrin: "Moses was educated in all the wisdom of the Egyptians and was powerful in speech and action" (Acts 7:22). He was powerful in speech? That's what the Good Book says. So what happened? When Moses failed and bailed, he went to the caboose and stayed there. Thought he deserved to be there. Got stuck there. He forgot his preordained preparation and his God-given ability.

Oh, I wish I were sitting right there with you and we could just chat and throw around ideas. For now, I'll just ask you this question and maybe one day we'll sit and talk long.

How do you think Moses came up with the idea that he was *not* a good speaker? Here's what I think: Moses came up with the idea by comparing himself to other people *he* thought were good speakers.

It's the same way with you and me. Comparison opens the door for sabotaging lies to steal our confidence, stymie our courage, and stand in the way of our calling. Comparison puts up roadblocks along the path to fulfilling our God-given destiny by setting an undefined standard of approval and acceptance.

We fear the REJECT stamp will come crashing down with wet ink that mars all of life. We fear that we are perhaps fatally flawed as confidence seeps through the holes of insecurity punctured and punctuated by comparison.

We compare our abilities to someone else's and come to this conclusion: *I could never do it like she does it.* And you know what? You were never meant to! God doesn't need two people just alike. He has uniquely and precisely created you with specific gifts and talents to do exactly what He has called you to do. So get good at being you!

David wrote, "For you created my inmost being; you knit me together in my mother's womb. I praise you because I am fearfully and wonderfully made; your works are wonderful, I *know that full well* (Ps. 139:13–14). He knew *what* full well? In these particular verses, David wasn't praising God for the way He flung the stars in the night sky, set the spinning earth on its axis, or stocked the oceans with sea creatures of every kind. David was marveling at the magnificent masterpiece called David. Me. You. He knew *that* full well.

You are God's workmanship. His masterpiece—His grand finale of all creation. Do you know *that* full well? You are amazing!

Paul wrote to the Galatians, "Make a careful exploration of who you are and the work you have been given, and then sink yourself into that. Don't be impressed with yourself. Don't compare yourself with others. Each of you must take responsibility for doing the creative best you can with your own life" (Gal. 6:4–5 Message).

Listen. If God didn't put it in you, then you don't need it to do what He has called you to do.

If God didn't make you eloquent, then you don't need to be eloquent to do what He's prepared for you to do.

If God didn't make you a good speller, then you don't need to be a good speller to do what He's prepared for you to do.

If God didn't place you in a home where you were the apple of your daddy's eye, then you don't need to be the apple of your daddy's eye to do all He has planned for you to do.

One pastor said, "One of the main reasons we struggle with insecurity is that we're comparing our behind-the-scenes with everybody else's highlight reel."[1] I promise to show you the film on the cutting room floor. See, I cut certain scenes out of my life's reel-to-reel, but God picked them back up, brushed them off, and inserted them back in. "These are some of My favorites," He explained. "The scenes you would rather no one see are the very ones that will help women see Me."

God knows your inadequacies and your insecurities. He knows what caused them and who caused them. He saw you before you even had them. Yet He chose you before you were born for a purpose—to fulfill a plan at a predetermined point in time (see Acts 17:26).

Comparison Hijacks Contentment

We live in a culture of constant comparison. Someone tweets that they just had lunch at a fab restaurant; you had canned tuna and raw carrots. Not even baby carrots but a big ol' carrot out of the bag. Someone posts an Instagram of a gaggle of friends dressed in Lilly Pulitzer pink and Tiffany blue lunching by the lake, and you're reading about it dressed in sweats, trudging down the grocery aisle with a snotty-nosed kid pawing at the cereal displays. You pull up Facebook and read about Barb's vacation in Paris, and you're happy for her . . . sorta. A woman looks at Pinterest boards and comes away with her greatest fears confirmed: her kids look shabby, her house looks dumpy, and her clothes look frumpy. Social media accentuates the culture of comparison by sending the false message that your monotonous, tedious, boring existence is a poor excuse for living compared to others whose lives are awesomely exciting all the time. Secretly you hope your husband never stumbles across Pinterest to realize what a loser of a wife he really has. Mercy!

Social media breeds instant comparison at the click of a button. Comparing who has more Facebook friends, retweets, followers, and re-pins is maddening. The age-old comparisons of appearance, accomplishments, possessions, and position are still around. Technology has simply magnified the access to other people's lives, even though you're only seeing what others want you to see.

Then there are Christmas letters. Photo cards of friends and family with letters detailing every wonderful milestone of the previous year. We read them and think, *My life stinks!* That letter doesn't tell about Brian getting suspended from school for cussing in the classroom, Megan getting caught lying about studying at a friend's house, Brie's ongoing battle with depression, Dad's loss of a major account, or Mom's twenty-pound weight gain. Just the highlights. Only the good stuff. We read it and say, "Good for them," all the while thinking, *What's wrong with me?*

Comparison is the devil's tool that he uses to undermine your confidence and kill contentment like nothing else ever will. It magnifies insecurities and fosters a self-absorbed preoccupation with your inadequacies. Bible teacher Beth Moore said, "In the dead of the night when insecurities crawl on us like fleas, all of us have terrifying bouts of insecurity and panics of insignificance. Our human natures pitifully fall to the temptation to pull out the tape measure and gauge ourselves against people who seem more gifted and anointed by God."[2]

Paul, like Moses, did not consider himself a very good speaker (1 Cor. 2:1; 2 Cor. 11:6). And he asked God to take away a particular weakness that constantly plagued him. We are never told what that "thorn in the flesh" was, and I'm glad. By not knowing, we can slip our own weakness right into God's promise. "But he said to me," Paul goes on to say, "'my grace is sufficient for you, for my power is made perfect in weakness.' Therefore I will boast all the more gladly about my weaknesses, so that Christ's power may rest on me" (2 Cor. 12:9).

Have you ever wondered why Jesus picked such a ragtag bunch of blundering, blubbering misfits to be His disciples? Even though they stumbled their way through much of the Gospels, once they were filled with the Holy Spirit, this uneducated, unrefined, untrained bunch of unruly fishermen changed the world. A few days after Pentecost, the Jewish supreme court questioned Peter and John about their persistence in preaching the gospel and their audacity to heal a beggar lame from birth.

The dynamic duo preached a mini-sermon that struck the religious rulers to the core. But here's my favorite part of the entire scenario: "When they saw the courage of Peter and John and realized that they were unschooled, ordinary men, they were astonished and they took note that these men had been with Jesus" (Acts 4:13).

The Sanhedrin leaders were mystified at how this bunch of scrappy, saw-toothed misfits could wax so eloquently. Then they had an aha moment. They realized the men had been with Jesus. That explained everything.

That's what I want people to say about me! "She's such an ordinary girl. How does she do what she does? Oh, I get it. She's been with Jesus!" Can you think of any better accolade? I sure can't.

Comparison sullies the canvas upon which God longs to display His greatest work. Nothing will rob you of your confidence in Christ like comparison. Let go of the tendency to compare and take hold of your uniquely fashioned, preordained, God-given talents and abilities. You are specifically equipped by God to do everything He has called you to do and to go through.

Make Every Effort

You've got what it takes to do all that God has prepared for you to do. As we've already seen, "His divine power has given us *everything we need* for a godly life through our knowledge of him who called us by his own glory and goodness" (2 Pet. 1:3). But that doesn't mean you get to sit back on your haunches and do nothing. Peter wrote, "For this very reason, *make every effort* to add to your faith goodness" (1:5). "Therefore, my brothers and sisters, *make every effort* to confirm your calling and election" (1:10). "*Make every effort* to be found spotless, blameless and at peace with him" (3:14).

Author Mark Buchanan said it well: "Those who do not make every effort are like the blind man whose sight is restored, but who never adjusts to that. He remains in his old ways, tapping his cane on the sidewalk, rattling his cup at the curb, reading by Braille, groping and shuffling, turning light into darkness, day into night."[3]

You have everything you need. You've got what it takes to do all that God has called you to do and to be. So now make every effort to do so—to take advantage of who you are, what you have, and where you are in Christ. Don't waste time comparing yourself to someone else. Sharpen your skills. Practice your trade. Exercise your gifts. Take hold of the truth and be on your way.

God had given Moses everything he needed for the task of leading the Israelites out of Egypt. He orchestrated events so Pharaoh's daughter would walk by the Nile at the precise moment baby Moses cried out from the floating basket. He choreographed Miriam's actions so she would witness the love-struck princess's rescue. God made sure Moses was raised in Pharaoh's household, learned the Egyptian culture, and mastered the Egyptian language. This was the Holy-Ghost prep school, and Moses was pre-enrolled before he was even born. But when he failed and bailed, Moses left bits and pieces of his confidence strewn along the path as he fled into the desert. By the time he reached Midian, it was all gone.

Oh, friend, the devil would like nothing more than to steal your confidence. Jesus reminds us, "The thief comes only to kill and steal and destroy" (John 10:10). There is no more perfect time for him to make his move than in a season of failure. All through life he is looking for opportunities to steal your confidence, stifle your conviction, and siphon your courage. And if that confidence is based on anything other than who you are, what you have, and where you are as a child of God, it can be easily snatched away. You can lose your job, your marriage, your children, your looks, your home, your money, and your position in the community. But if your confidence is firmly grounded in Jesus Christ, you will not be shaken. That's not to say that it is easy.

The writer of Hebrews encourages us, "So do not throw away your confidence; it will be richly rewarded" (10:35).

When you stand firm on your identity in Christ, you will be unshakable.

When you move forward in the power of Christ, you will be unstoppable.

When you experience difficult circumstances yet trust in the sovereignty of God, you will be unbreakable.

When you fall into the trap of comparison and come up lacking, consider what Jesus did for you on that rough-hewn cross—the nails, the thorns, the side-piercing sword. Jesus is proof that you have great worth to God. The fact that He created you to be His image-bearer renders you incapable of insignificance, no matter what has been done to you or through you in this life.

An Audience of One

It was my first major speaking engagement back in the nineties. Why I had agreed to do it was beyond me. I had never stood up in front of more than a handful of women at my Bible study or our church's women's retreat. Even then, I didn't have to use a microphone. And now, five hundred expectant women were going to be staring at me. To top it all off, the theme was "Unshakable Confidence in Christ." Laughable.

Two weeks before the event, I attended a luncheon where my mentor, Mary Marshall Young, was going to be sharing a short devotion. It was in a prestigious part of town I did not frequent. One of those gatherings where the women's purses and shoes matched, and by that I mean they were made out of the same material. I was so uncomfortable as I slid onto my toile-covered chair and placed my Walmart purse under the table. *And where is Mary Marshall anyway?* I wondered. Oh, my word, she waved at me from another table across the room and left me to swim in the mermaid-infested waters alone.

The other ladies at the table all knew each other and began bantering back and forth. One just about swooned as she said, "What did you think about the speaker at our church's last women's event? Wasn't he wonderful?"

"Oh yes," her friend replied. "He was so powerfully anointed! One of the best speakers I have ever heard. What a testimony!"

"I cried all the way through his story," another chimed in. "Oh, how God worked mightily in his family."

"And then Pastor invited him to speak on Sunday morning! I don't think we'll ever have a speaker as good as that one again."

They went on and on describing this amazing man of God with words like *anointed, formidable, dynamic, electric,* and *articulate.*

"Where do you ladies attend church?" I asked, trying to contribute to the conversation.

When they answered, my little tea sandwich lodged in my throat and my heart flip-flopped in my chest. This was the same church where I was booked to speak in two weeks. To these same women!

I never mentioned to the ladies that I was going to be the speaker for their next women's night out, because at that moment, I wasn't so sure I would be. I have no idea what Mary Marshall said in her devotion. All I wanted to do was grab my Walmart purse and escape the scene.

When the event was over, I lickety-split power-walked to my car as fast as I could without looking like I was running. With my face set like flint, I drove over to that church. All the while, Satan was whispering in my ear, "Who do you think you are, going to speak at that church? Did you hear the caliber of people they bring in? That man came all the way from across the country. You are just coming from across town. What could you possibly have to say to these women that would make any difference? If I were you, I'd bow out now before I embarrassed myself."

And you know what? Even though I knew it was the devil talking, I believed him. After all, what he was saying made a lot more sense than the "My New Identity in Christ" list posted on my refrigerator door.

"Excuse me," I said to the church receptionist once I arrived. "I'd like to purchase a tape of the speaker you had for your last women's event."

"Oh sure, honey. He was really great."

"Yes, I heard."

"Here you go. That will be five dollars."

I went out to the car, popped the tape into the console, pressed play, and braced myself for an hour of power.

I heard nothing.

Pressed fast-forward. Pressed play. There was nothing.

Flipped the tape over. Pressed play. There was nothing.

Pressed fast-forward on side two. Pressed play. There was nothing.

The tape was blank.

Then God spoke to my heart.

Sharon, you do not need to hear what My servant said to these people two weeks ago. The tape is blank because I do not want you to compare yourself to anyone else. It doesn't matter what he said. I gave him a message. I will give you a message. I can speak through a prophet, I can speak through a fisherman, and I can speak through a donkey.

Who are you "performing" for, My child, them or Me? Do not compare yourself to anyone. You are My child and I am asking you to speak to an audience of One.

I didn't bother getting my money back for the defective tape. It was exactly what I needed to hear.

So next time Satan taunted me with the words "Who do you think you are?" I replied:

I am the bride of Christ.

I am a co-heir with Christ.

I am a chosen, holy, dearly loved child of God.

I am more than a conqueror through Christ.

I am a temple of God. His Spirit lives in me.

I am blessed with every spiritual blessing in the heavenlies.

I have the power of the Holy Spirit in me and working through me to do all things God has called me to do.

And who are you?

nine

Get Up and Get Going

*Let Go of Debilitating Discouragement
and Take Hold of Your Next Assignment*

My bags were packed. My passport was up to date. My feet were itching to get started.

For over a year, my husband and I had planned a trip to Italy, Greece, and Turkey with six of our closest friends. We had plotted our course, prepared for our travel, and saved our pennies. This was a big deal for us—for me. I was going to stand on the very mount in Athens where Paul preached one of my favorite verses: "In him we live and move and have our being" (Acts 17:28). We were going to explore the catacombs where some of our very first brothers and sisters in Christ were buried and walk the very steps of Paul in Ephesus.

When the day finally arrived, we flew to Rome to spend three days before setting sail to Greece. Rome did not disappoint: the Coliseum, the Appian Way, the aqueducts, and the catacombs. I had to pinch myself to make sure I was really there.

The night before boarding the ship, I celebrated by eating some local fish that was a little too fishy. In the wee hours of the morning, my body commenced rejecting the contents of my digestive system in every unpleasant way possible. I'd experienced this before. I knew what it was. Food poisoning.

Being a good trouper, I crawled into the shuttle van the next morning with our band of explorers, closed my eyes, and proceeded to the ship terminal for the next leg of our journey. We arrived at the dock and joined the throng of other vacationers being herded through the roped check-in lanes. One of the attendants handed me a short form to complete for admittance. And there it was. The question.

"Have you experienced vomiting in the past forty-eight hours?"

I looked at the paper.

I looked at my carefree, expectant friends.

I looked at the beckoning ship with my name on it.

I looked at my wary husband—questioning without a word.

I took a deep breath.

I checked "yes."

When I handed my boarding papers to the customer service representative, she took one look at the box checked "yes" and spoke through a forced smile. "Ma'am, please step aside," she said with a thick Italian accent. "I'll be back in a moment."

A few minutes later, the ship nurse appeared. She took my temperature and asked me to please move to another area of the terminal. I explained to her about the fishy fish, the food poisoning, and the dehydration that caused my temperature to be elevated one degree. I explained that I had experienced food poisoning before and knew without a shadow of a doubt that was what I had. She just nodded, took a few notes, and then disappeared into the belly of the ship.

After twenty minutes or so, she returned. "I'm sorry, ma'am," she began, "you cannot board this ship. You have been denied passage.

You are not fit to sail. We cannot take the risk that you will infect the other passengers. You need to go home."

Let that sink in for just a moment. You are "not fit to sail." You have been "denied passage." You need to "go home."

Steve and I were crushed as our brokenhearted friends walked across the gangplank, disappeared into the ship's hull, and sailed away without us.

Have you ever been in a similar situation? Maybe not being denied passage on the trip of a lifetime, but perhaps being rejected by an employer, a project manager, or a publisher? A broken engagement. A crumbled marriage. A wayward child. A negative pregnancy test. A sudden death. A shattered dream.

Perhaps you've prepared, planned, and prayed. You can almost reach out and touch your ship, almost taste the salty air of success, almost feel the gentle sway of passage. But then someone whose opinion matters shows up and declares that you are "not fit to sail." They deny you passage on the ship you know was meant for you and tell you to "go home." *They* decide, "It's over."

Perhaps you've felt the gut-wrenching disappointment of rejection. The heart-crushing discouragement of apparent failure. The realization that life has just not turned out like you thought it would. If so, you're not alone.

The Expectation Gap

Discouragement comes when there is a gap between what you expect and what you experience—when there is a gap between what you *hoped* would happen and what actually *does* happen. Discouragement can destroy your passion and undermine your purpose. It can take root because of what others say or didn't say—a mom who said too much, a dad who said too little. Unmet expectations can become the breeding ground for discouragement to multiply and take root.

We certainly see that in Moses's life. When he was forty years old, he expected to be the deliverer for his people. But what he experienced was rejection and regret. In his last effort to pass on this assignment, Moses argued,

> Pardon your servant, Lord. I have never been eloquent, neither in the past nor since you have spoken to your servant. I am slow of speech and tongue. (Exod. 4:10)

This statement that came from Moses's stuttering lips was simply not true. As Stephen reminded us, "Moses was educated in all the wisdom of the Egyptians and was powerful in speech and action" (Acts 7:22). Moses had defined himself by his failure and was held hostage by a constant state of discouragement.

Discouragement causes many a believer to pull up a lounge chair in cul-de-sac Christianity and refuse to venture out to the adventurous faith. They mumble the words "Fool me once, shame on you; fool me twice, shame on me" over their hopes and dreams. They fill the gap between what they hope for and what they experience with the false belief that dreams aren't worth the effort.

What we tend to see as a permanent condition, God sees as a temporary situation. What you see as one of your greatest setbacks might be one of God's incredible setups for marvelous miracles to occur. If you are meeting resistance in your hopes and dreams, then you're most likely on the right track. The devil wouldn't mess with you if you weren't a menace to his plans and a valuable asset to God.

What the devil really wants to do is to steal your confidence, and the best time to rob you blind is during a season of disappointment. Guard your heart. Don't be caught unaware and allow him to hold you back, trip you up, or slow you down. The circumstances are, well, just circumstantial—collateral damage in the real battle to take away your confidence in Christ.

The Disappointment of Shattered Dreams

Everyone will experience discouragement at some point in life. It will look as different and unique as the fingerprints on your hands, but disappointments will come.

Dropping your son off at a rehab center instead of college.

Signing divorce papers instead of planning an anniversary party.

Looking for a job rather than getting a raise.

Cuddling up with a good book rather than cozying up with a good husband.

Planning a funeral instead of planning a future.

Counting out food stamps instead of writing a check.

Moving up in your career rather than rocking a baby in your arms.

Yes, everyone will experience broken dreams at some point in their life.

I had a dream of having a house full of giggling little girls and boisterous, rowdy boys. After Steven was born, I thought we were well on our way to making that dream a reality. I loved being a mom! With Bambi-length eyelashes, chubby cheeks, and a shock of black hair (which later turned blond), Steven had my heart in his tiny little fist the first time I laid eyes on him.

Eighteen months later, I was ready to plan for baby number two. We had conceived Steven with no trouble whatsoever, so I thought giving him a sibling would be just as easy. We told Steven, "Mommy and Daddy are asking God to give you a little brother or sister!" The plan was that Steven would see how God answers prayer. At the end of our family prayer each night, Steven would add, "And, God, please give Mommy and Daddy another Jaynes baby."

But the next month there was no news of another Jaynes baby. Or the next . . . or the next. Months turned into years, and Steven continued to pray, "And, God, please give Mommy and Daddy another Jaynes baby. Amen."

Doctor visits, infertility treatment, and monthly heartbreak consumed my thinking. This is not how the story was supposed to go. The disappointment was crushing. The discouragement was visceral.

Steven was just about to turn five and he was still praying the prayer for a brother or sister every night. It looked like we were not going to have more children, but I didn't know what to tell this little towheaded boy so full of faith. How do you tell a kid he doesn't need to pray a certain prayer anymore? Should I even do that? Was this seemingly unanswered prayer going to damage his faith?

"God, if this is Your will for our family," I said with a sigh, "You've got to take care of this prayer situation with Steven."

We had a miniature table and chairs in the kitchen where Steven and I ate lunch together each day. One day while we were sharing peanut butter and jelly sandwiches, Steven looked up and in his sweet little voice said, "Mommy, have you ever thought that maybe God wants you to have only one Jaynes baby?"

"Yes, I have thought that. And if that's the case, I'm so thankful He has given me all I have ever hoped for wrapped up in one package: *you!*"

Then he cocked his little head and said, "Well, what I think we ought to do is keep praying until you're too old to have one. Then we'll know that's His answer!"

What a great idea. The truth is, I had been worried about Steven's faith, but all the while, it was my own that was suffering. I was so discouraged that I was having trouble believing God truly loved me.

Steven didn't know how old too old was, but with a childlike faith he did know God could do anything. If God's answer was no, Steven didn't have a problem with that. I told him no many times, and he understood that no did not mean, "I don't love you." No just meant, "No, because I am your parent and I know what's best for you."

Several years after Steven's bold declaration, the miracle happened. I discovered I was pregnant. While Steve and I had resigned ourselves to raising Steven as an only child, it appeared God had another plan after all.

Doctor visits confirmed that the baby was growing, healthy, and strong. But into the second trimester, something went wrong and the baby died. Her heart stopped beating, and in a way, so did mine.

I wish I could tell you I got out my Bible and began reciting the verses about my new identity. I wish I could tell you I quoted "All things work together for good" and kept my chin up. I wish I could tell you I clung to the words of Romans 8:28, but I did not. I climbed into bed and pulled the covers over my empty womb and my empty heart. "If this is how You love me," I cried, "then forget it." Then I gave God the silent treatment, as if I could somehow pay Him back.

I was mad. I was hurt. I felt betrayed by the One who was supposed to love me most. Discouragement set up camp and I drove the tent pegs in deep. I avoided church, stayed away from happy people, and allowed my grief to bring my life to a screeching halt. I listened to the lies of Satan as he whispered, "I told you so. God doesn't love you. You can't trust Him."

Ann Voskamp wrote, "I wonder . . . if the rent in the canvas of our life's backdrop, the losses that puncture our world, our own emptiness, might actually become places to see. To see through to God."[1] This was a see-through place, but until I opened my eyes, I would not see God.

In *A Sudden Glory: God's Lavish Response to Your Ache for Something More*, I wrote:

> Could it be that the puncture wounds in the canvas of your life—the losses, the disappointments, the crushing blows—might actually become the rent places of the soul through which you can see God? Through which you can peer beyond your earthly trappings

into glory moments beyond? Through which you can see His light bursting through the opening? I believe they *could* be. . . .

When we experience shattered dreams, broken relationships, tragic losses or unfulfilled longings—when we face the varied levels of disappointment it can be difficult to feel God's presence, to see His hand, and to hear His voice. . . . That doesn't mean that God is not there. It only means that the sadness in our own hearts has drawn the shades and locked the doors. We question whether or not we even want to live in union with God if this is where the path leads. We tend to wriggle out of His arms like an angry child or slip out of His embrace like a disgruntled lover, all the while hoping He will pull us back in and tell us that we have simply misunderstood.[2]

Turning "Why Me?" into "What Now?"

We've already looked at Philippians 3:13–14: "But one thing I do: Forgetting what is behind and straining toward what is ahead, I press on toward the goal to win the prize for which God has called me heavenward in Christ Jesus." But does this apply to the disappointments and discouraging circumstances in our lives as well as what has been done to us and through us? I believe it does.

No, I will never forget the pain of losing a child. But I have chosen not to allow the pain of disappointment to hold me hostage in depression and anger. To live free and move forward in our faith—to experience all that God has for us this side of heaven—we must relinquish disappointments to God and allow Him to fill the expectation gap with more of Himself. We stop saying "Why me?" and start saying "What now?"

A few years after the loss of this much-wanted child, I read the Song of Solomon during my quiet time with God. On this particular day, I was reading this romantic pursuit as if I were the bride and Jesus were the groom. "I am a rose of Sharon," the bride proclaimed (Song of Sol. 2:1). Struck by the mention of my name,

I looked up "Sharon" in my Bible dictionary. I discovered it was a fertile valley near Mount Carmel in the Holy Land.

At that moment, God whispered to my heart: *Your medical records may have the word* infertile *stamped on the chart, but I have named you "fertile valley." You do not have a house full of children—your dream did not turn out the way you thought it would—but I have given you spiritual children all around the world.* At that moment, I realized that through writing, speaking, and simply obeying the nudges of God to reach out to one of His own, He has allowed me to give birth to many children and nurture them as well. When we let go of the disappointment and take hold of God's appointment by moving forward, life will unfold in ways unimaginable to the human mind.

The enemy would like nothing better than for a discouraged child of God to get stuck in the muck and mire of self-pity, self-deprecation, and self-dejection. *Why did God allow this to happen? I thought He loved me? I give up! This isn't worth it! Where was God? Where is God now?*

The truth is, sometimes life doesn't seem fair. To the untrained eye, there is a lopsidedness and randomness to the distribution of windfalls and pitfalls. But the soul who sees beyond the external and has the courage to reach beyond sight experiences a trusting calm that is impossible to explain.

Don't pitch a tent in your discouragement. Instead, take the next step forward. Turn your "Why me?" into "What now?" and listen for the next great adventure.

Recognize the Way Out

All through the Bible we see men and women held hostage by discouragement. Naomi was discouraged because her husband and two sons had died, leaving her in a foreign land to fend for herself. She even went as far as changing her name from Naomi, which means "pleasant," to Mara, which means "bitter."

Jonah was so discouraged when God did not destroy the repentant Ninevites that he laid down under a gourd vine and wanted to die. The Samaritan woman was so discouraged over her five failed marriages that she drew water during the heat of the day just to avoid the gossiping women who gathered theirs in the mornings. The disciples were so discouraged over the death of Jesus on the cross that they hid in an upper room, not knowing what to do with the rest of their lives.

In each one of these examples, God offered a way out of the doldrums of discouragement. He sent Ruth to help Naomi remember that she served a God who had not forgotten her. He sent Jonah a gourd-eating worm to teach him the value of human lives. He sent Jesus to show the Samaritan woman that her life wasn't hopeless but full of promise. The resurrected Jesus appeared to the despondent disciples and assured them the greatest story of all time was not over, not by a long shot.

Get Up and Get Going

A few years after the Israelites made it to the Promised Land, they grew tired of being ruled by God through the prophets. They wanted to have a king like all the other nations. Samuel was the ruling prophet at the time, and he told the people all the reasons having a king was a bad idea. They persisted in their demands, and eventually God allowed them to choose a king. "They are not rejecting you," God assured Samuel. "They are rejecting Me."

The people picked Saul because he was tall, dark, and handsome. I'm not kidding. It's right there in black and white. Saul reluctantly accepted the kingship, was anointed by the Holy Spirit, and totally depended on God for his new position. But after a while, Saul decided being a king wasn't so hard after all. He disobeyed and dishonored God by taking matters into his own hands. As a result, God snatched away Saul's kingship and removed his anointing.

Samuel was so discouraged over Saul's failure that he went to bed and pulled the covers up over his head. The very person he was in charge of had turned away from God. He was disappointed in Saul, and he felt sorry for himself.

Now this is important. If I were sitting right there with you, I'd stand up in a chair and read this out loud. Here we go. One day God said, "How long will you mourn for Saul, since I have rejected him as king over Israel?" (1 Sam. 16:1). I love Eugene Peterson's paraphrase: "So, how long are you going to mope over Saul?" (Message).

Mope. Yep. That's a good word.

God asks you and me the same question: *How long will you mope because life hasn't turned out like you thought it would? How long?* He could have said the same words to Moses.

I don't mean to make little of any of the painful or discouraging situations in your life. But I do know this: no matter how painful or discouraging the circumstances of life may be, God never intends for you to get stuck there. You should never put a period where God puts a comma. There's always more of your story to be written. When you loosen the string holding the binding of your book tightly shut and give God a free hand to continue the narrative of your life, things the eye has not seen and the ear has not heard and have not entered the mind of man will be yours.

God goes on to say to Samuel, "Fill your horn with oil and *be on your way*; I am sending you to Jesse of Bethlehem. I have chosen one of his sons to be king" (1 Sam. 16:1).

At some point in our moping about, God comes to us and says, "Enough already. Get up. Get going. Be on your way. I've got something for you to do. Your life is not over. The story has more chapters to be written. Let go of your discouragement and take hold of the next adventure I have planned for you."

The question is, What will you say?

Samuel was very reluctant to get out of bed. He wasn't thrilled about God's next adventure to put oil in his horn and head out to anoint the next king of Israel. "I can't do that," Samuel replied. "Saul will hear about it and kill me."

Then God answered, "Take a heifer with you and say, 'I have come to sacrifice to the LORD.' Invite Jesse to the sacrifice, *and I will show you what to do.* You are to anoint for me the one I indicate" (1 Sam. 16:2–3).

I will show you what to do. Does that sound familiar? God said to Moses, "I will teach you what to say. I will tell you what to do." And that's all God expects of me and of you—take the first step of obedience. Get up and get going. He will take care of the rest.

"Samuel did what the LORD said" (1 Sam. 16:4). Ah, the key to experiencing the adventurous life of a thriving faith—the faith you always longed for.

Move Forward in the Dark

Sometimes you expect you're getting a Rachel and you wake up with a Leah. Okay, I know that example might connect better with a guy, but you get the point. Let me try that again. What do you do after you've crossed the Red Sea of obstacles only to be dying of thirst at Marah three days later? How do you keep your dancing from turning into disappointment? One thing is for sure: you don't drive down your tent pegs by the disappointing waters of Marah and camp out there. You move on.

I think of the women on Jesus's ministry team. They had committed their lives to the Messiah and believed He would restore Israel. Mary Magdalene and a handful of other women had followed Him for over three years. But life had not turned out like they thought it would. Their hopes and dreams were nailed to a cross and the lifeblood spilled on the ground to be trampled underfoot. Their future lay in a borrowed tomb—sealed behind an imposing stone.

It appeared Jesus was not going to be the ruler and set things right after all. The very people He came to save had killed Him. This was not how the story was supposed to go . . . at least in their eyes.

So what did Mary and the other women do? On the third day after Jesus's death, *while it was still dark*, they got up, gathered their spices, and started walking to the tomb. Never mind that it was still dark. Never mind that a giant boulder blocked the tomb's entrance, a stone too heavy for the women to move. Never mind that armed Roman soldiers stood guard over the grave. Never mind that the disciples were so discouraged and disillusioned that they hid away in a secret room. Never mind all that. The women didn't have all the details worked out in their heads, but they were not going to sit home in their discouragement, paralyzed into inactivity. They were going to move forward . . . *while it was still dark*.

Mary Magdalene got up, and she got going . . . *while it was still dark*. In the end, she was not disappointed that she took this step of faith, and you won't be either. Just as assuredly as Jesus met her at her greatest point of need, He will meet you at yours.

Did you notice that Mary Magdalene didn't wait until her circumstances changed before she got moving? Jesus was still dead as far as she knew. But she got up and moved forward anyway. And where did she go? Yes, she went to the tomb, but there is more. She went back to the last place she had seen Him. Perhaps that is where you need to go today. Go back to the last place you encountered Jesus. Even if it is still dark. Even if you are still in a dark place. Even if a seemingly impossibly imposing boulder of disappointment is blocking your dreams. Don't worry about moving the stone. God's good at that. You just keep putting one faithful foot in front of the other and let God take care of the rest.

Oh, what we miss when we make camp in the painful place of disappointment and refuse God's invitation to continue the adventurous journey. We miss the moments of sudden glory when our eyes are shut tight because of discouragement and our hearts are bolted fast with despair.

Don't allow the weight of discouragement to hold you down or lower your expectations of the life in Christ. Get up. Get moving. Open your eyes. Open your heart. There's more to experience just around the bend.

Fit to Sail

What do you do when your ship pulls up anchor and sails off without you? How do you respond when life doesn't turn out like you thought it would? Where do you turn when the powers that be toss your hopes and dreams overboard and tell you to go home? What do you do when someone whose opinion matters denies you passage on the boat you were meant to board? The answers to those questions can change everything. You need to decide right now—before it happens.

Let's go back to the story at the beginning of this chapter—to the trip that ended before it began. Pull up a chair and sit with me in the seaport terminal as we watched our friends sail away without us. That's what Nicoletta did. She was a young woman who worked for the cruise line and seemed just as brokenhearted as we felt. "I wish I should help you," she whispered in awkward English.

She sat with me. Tried to console me. And cared for me. Then she came up with a crazy idea.

"I know this would be a lot of trouble," she began. "I know this would be risky and costly. But what you could do is take a ninety-minute cab ride back to Rome, check into a hotel by the airport, and book a flight from Rome to Reggio Calabria for tomorrow

170

morning at 6:00 a.m. Once in Reggio, take a bus from the airport to the seaport terminal. Then take a ferry from the seaport terminal, across the Mediterranean, to the island of Sicily, where the ship will be docked tomorrow. When you get to Sicily, find a local doctor who will examine you. If the doctor declares you healthy and writes you a certificate saying you are 'fit to sail,' you can then take that back to the ship doctor and perhaps he will allow you to board. But you have to do all that before 3:00 p.m. tomorrow when the ship will leave Messina and set sail for Greece."

That was the craziest idea we had ever heard. Who did she think we were, Superman and Wonder Woman? So what did we do?

We took a cab back to Rome and booked a room by the airport for the night. At 6:00 a.m. the next morning we took a flight to Reggio Calabria, Italy. From the airport we took a bus to the Reggio sea terminal and then a ferry across the Mediterranean to the island of Sicily. Once in Sicily we met up with Nicoletta's friend Lucia, who drove us to her personal doctor, who spoke no English. The doctor poked, prodded, and prepared a report that declared I was healthy and "fit to sail." The report was in Italian, so Lucia translated it into English using her Smartphone app. The doctor signed the document, put her official stamp on it, and we exchanged double-cheek kisses . . . three times. She felt so sorry for us and all we had gone through over the past twenty-four hours that she wouldn't even accept payment. More double-cheek kisses. More tears.

Steve and I scurried back to that cruise ship, waving the official "fit to sail" document like the victory flag it was. The attendant gave it to the ship's doctor, who then allowed us to board the ship at 2:45. Fifteen minutes later, the ship's horn blasted, announcing it was leaving the port.

Did that story make you tired? It makes me tired just thinking about it. But here's what you need to know. At some point in your life, someone whose opinion you think matters might tell you to "go home." They may deny you passage on a ship you know is meant for you. They may tell you:

You are not smart enough.

You don't have the right resources.

Your writing is not good enough.

You don't have the right credentials.

Your past is too sordid.

Your idea is not practical.

You might even stand on the dock of your precisely prepared hopes and dreams and watch as your friends get on the ship you long to board—without you. All you can do is put on a forced smile and wish them well, when what you want more than anything is to jump onto that ship and say, "You've made a mistake. This is my boat! It was meant for me too! Don't leave me!"

And if that happens to you, you will have a choice. You can give up and go home. Or you can do what you need to, to get on board. You can take a cab, take a flight, take a bus, take a ferry, and do whatever you need to do to get on the ship God has prepared for you. Let go of discouragement and take hold of your God-given dream. If you hit a wall, climb over it. I pray you'll unearth dreams you've buried in the soil of discouragement and disappointment. Dust them off. Move forward. Live bold.

Pressing on in the face of discouragement might seem a bit crazy. Persevering when the world puts a "Do Not Enter" sign in front of your hopes and dreams takes a determination that is not for the faint of heart. Relentlessly pursuing your passion when what you'd really like to do is crawl back into bed and cry will try your stamina. But the alternative is to go home and wave as others sail away while you cozy up with the remote.

I don't know what your ship is today. I don't know what God has planned for you, but I do know it is something good.

I often hear people say, "I'm waiting for my ship to come in." I haven't known anyone whose "ship has come in." But I have known a lot of people who have "made every effort" by working hard to get on the ship God has prepared for them. And I've known a lot of people who've watched their ship sail away because they gave up too soon, because they decided the work was too hard, or because they settled for being a victim of someone's opinion rather than a victor over discouragement, disillusionment, and dejection.

History is full of untold stories of men and women who did not complete their assignments from God but stopped too soon in the face of disappointment. Perseverance is fueled by moving beyond the circumstances that are seemingly against you with confidence in the Holy Spirit who is within you.

Pressing on in the shadow of discouragement is hard work. Giving up is easier. But those who persist in the shadow of disappointment experience the sweetness of success. They are the ones who live the adventurous faith God intended all along. The ones who live *bold*.

Final Words from the Fiery Bush

In the end, Moses begged God to send someone else to speak to Pharaoh and lead the Israelites out of Egypt. And while God's anger burned against Moses for his lack of faith, He wasn't surprised. "What about your brother, Aaron the Levite?" God replied. "I know he can speak well. *He is already on his way* to meet you, and he will be glad to see you" (Exod. 4:14).

He is already on his way. God knew how the conversation would end. Midian was a three-day journey from Egypt, which means Aaron had left a couple of days before the holy spark had even ignited the bush.

Aaron tagging along was not God's best. He caused a cauldron of trouble. And this gives me pause. I wonder what God allows because of my reluctance to leave the comfort of cul-de-sac Christianity, my unwillingness to move from my place of complacent stuck-ness, my heel-digging refusal to heed His call. I wonder.

Never once do we see that Moses doubted God. He didn't doubt what God could do; what he did doubt was that God could do it through him. So many times I've spoken about, written about, and taught that the reason we flounder in our faith is because we don't trust God enough. But for most of us, that is not really true. It is not that we doubt God; it is that we doubt He would work mightily for *us*—work mightily through *us*.

But when we say yes to God in spite of our perceived inadequacies, miracles happen, walls come crashing down, the Promised Land gate flies open. Sometimes God allows you to see the results of your obedience; other times they remain hidden until heaven. But the treasures forged in the furnace of obedience are always there.

ten

One Rock Is All You Need

*Let Go of Timid Reluctance
and Take Hold of Bold Believing*

So what are you going to do when God calls your name? When He taps you on the shoulder and says, "Now's the time"?

There was a kid in the Bible who had the right idea. Let me introduce you to him.

In chapter 9, we met up with the prophet Samuel and saw how God urged him to let go of his disappointment and move forward in his new assignment. "Fill your horn with oil and be on your way," God told him. "I am sending you to Jesse of Bethlehem. I have chosen one of his sons to be king" (1 Sam. 16:1).

Then one of my favorite verses: "Samuel did what the LORD said" (1 Sam. 16:4). He traveled to the town of Bethlehem, to the house of Jesse, and asked to see his sons. When they paraded by for inspection, Samuel was impressed with the eldest right away. Eliab was tall, dark, and handsome.

But the LORD said to Samuel, "Do not consider his appearance or his height, for I have rejected him. The LORD does not look at the things people look at. People look at the outward appearance, but the LORD looks at the heart."

Then Jesse called Abinadab and had him pass in front of Samuel. But Samuel said, "The LORD has not chosen this one either." Jesse then had Shammah pass by, but Samuel said, "Nor has the LORD chosen this one." (1 Sam. 7–9)

Seven sons. Seven rejections. I'm sure about this time Samuel was scratching his head. Confused, he turned to Jesse and asked, "Is this all your sons?"

Then, as if it were an afterthought, Jesse muttered, "Oh yeah, I do have another son. I forgot all about him. His name is David—my youngest. He's out taking care of the sheep."

Samuel then said, "Send for him; we will not sit down until he arrives" (v. 11).

They didn't take a knee, take a seat, or take a break. They stood and waited while the *Jeopardy* theme song played in the background.

And in walks young David—a smelly, inexperienced, unqualified kid who was probably around thirteen years old.

Then the Lord said, "Rise and anoint him; this is the one" (v. 12).

So right there in the presence of David's older brothers, Samuel anoints this boy to be the next king of Israel.

David was the littlest.

The least.

The loneliest.

But in God's eyes, David was chosen.

Anointed.

Appointed.

God chose David. God chose Moses. God has chosen you. He is saying to you right now, "You are the one!"

Consider this: David was so insignificant to his own family

that his father didn't even bring him into the house when Samuel asked to see all of his sons. At least he could have invited him in to watch. But even though he was forgotten or at least ignored by his family, David was the very one God chose for a great purpose and a wonderful plan. From that moment on, David was anointed by the power of the Holy Spirit for God's purpose that was yet to unfold.

Now, David was handsome too. Yes, Scripture does make mention of his "fine appearance and handsome features" (1 Sam. 16:12). But God made sure we knew his anointing had nothing to do with his physical appearance and everything to do with his heart.

I don't know what your childhood was like. Perhaps you felt insignificant or ignored by your parents or siblings. Perhaps you have experienced rejection by your friends, classmates, or co-workers. But make no mistake about it, God has chosen you. You! "For [God] *chose* [*you*] in him before the creation of the world to be holy and blameless in his sight" (Eph. 1:4).

Not only has God chosen you to be His child, but He has also appointed you to be an ambassador of Christ and bear fruit in His name. Jesus said, "You did not choose me, but I chose you and *appointed* you so that you might go and bear fruit—fruit that will last—and so that whatever you ask in my name the Father will give you" (John 15:16; see also 2 Cor. 5:20).

And like David, you have been anointed, not with oil but with the power of the Holy Spirit to do everything God has called you to do. "[God] *anointed* [*you*], set his seal of ownership on [*you*], and put his Spirit in [*your* heart] as a deposit, guaranteeing what is to come" (2 Cor. 1:21–22).

Hone Your Skills

Yes, David was chosen, anointed, and appointed as the next king of Israel. However, he didn't get to wear the royal robe on his shoulders, don the golden crown on his head, or slip the king's signet ring on his finger. He turned around and went right back out to those smelly sheep.

See, David had lessons to learn, lions to conquer, bears to fight, courage to forge, confidence to build. Make no mistake about it, David was still king, but he wasn't quite ready to take the throne. He was being made fit to reign as king in the field of everyday life. All the while, God was preparing David for what He had prepared for him. But even among the sheep, David was still king. He knew he didn't have anything to prove to anyone.

Perhaps that's where you are right now. You've been chosen, anointed, and appointed to live bold for God. But right now, you might be taking care of a few sheep of your own. Sheep with pink hair bows, dirty tennis shoes, and driver's permits. God might be developing your character, teaching you how to depend on Him, trust in Him, and rely upon Him. It is through seemingly insignificant acts of faithful obedience that God hones your abilities and prepares you for what He has prepared for you. We are made fit in our faith in the field of everyday life. Even though the crown is not on your head, you are still royalty (1 Pet. 2:9). You don't have a thing to prove to anyone. God said it. He meant it.

After David was anointed to be the next king, he didn't sit back and do nothing. He didn't say, "Well, I'm the king! Let the people come to me. I'm not going to go back there and take care of those stupid sheep!" He didn't develop a haughty attitude after Samuel anointed him. He didn't trade in his shepherd's staff for the king's scepter and refuse to head back to the pasture. He simply continued working at his present assignment and waited on God's timing. He honed his shepherding skills and got really good at it. We'll see just how good in a minute.

I'm reminded of nineteen-year-old Joey Prusak, who worked at a Dairy Queen in Hopkins, Minnesota, serving up ice cream and hamburgers all day. Some might not think that is an exciting job.

But it is not the job that defines you; it's what you do in the job that matters. One day a blind customer dropped a $20 bill when he was struggling to find his pocket and put his change away. A woman behind him picked up the money and put it in her pocket. Joey asked the woman to return the money to its rightful owner. She refused and said it was hers. Joey then asked the woman to leave the restaurant, as he would not serve someone so disrespectful.

The woman got extremely angry and swore at Joey before she left, but he remained calm. After the blind man had taken his food and sat down to eat, Joey went over to him, opened his own wallet, and gave the man $20 of his own money, two hours of pay. "I'm giving you $20 on behalf of myself and Dairy Queen," Joey said.

A customer who witnessed the exchange was so impressed with Joey's integrity, professionalism, and kindness that she wrote an email to Dairy Queen's corporate office praising his actions. "I was in shock by the generosity that your employee had, taking his own money out of his own wallet to give to the customer because some other lady decided to steal something that wasn't hers," the customer wrote. "I would proudly like to say that Joey has forever sealed my fate as a lifelong customer of the Mainstreet Dairy Queen. Thank you for outstanding customer service and for an even better experience."

In response, CEO and president John Gainor said, "We applaud [his] integrity, kindness and compassion. He is an inspiration to us all."

Later, Joey heard from Warren Buffett, whose company owns the ice-cream chain. Buffett invited Joey to an international business meeting and offered to fly him out on his private jet.[1] Another day a woman visited Dairy Queen and handed Prusak an envelope of money, saying it was for his college fund. Then a man from a nearby town dropped by the store and anonymously gave him five times what Joey had given the blind man. Prusak was on the Glenn Beck radio show, and Beck offered to buy a Dairy Queen franchise for Prusak to run. Prusak wasn't sure how serious Beck was, but as NPR reported, "He knows he's got a lot of options to weigh."[2]

Joey was just out taking care of sheep. He was doing the job assigned to him at the time, and he did it with excellence. I'm convinced God has more in store for Joey. Just like He had more in store for David. Just like He has more in store for you.

We need to take an assessment of the gifts and talents God has given us and develop them. Moses had forgotten all that God had already done to get him into position. He had forgotten about being saved by his mother's initiative and the princess's mercy. He had forgotten about being raised and educated in the ways of the Egyptians. He had forgotten all that God had done to prepare him for what He had prepared for him.

I don't think David forgot any of that. He simply continued on with what God had called him to do at the time, and he did it very well.

Get Ready

The next time we hear from David, four years have passed, and he's still taking care of sheep. He did get a part-time job playing the harp for King Saul when he had a bad headache, but he is still basically a dirty, smelly shepherd. And make no mistake about it, the harp gig was no accident either. You don't get to play the harp for the king just because you know how to pluck a few strings. He must have practiced and become one of the best harpists around to get the job. Again, he worked at the gifts God had given him.

Then one day David's father called him in from the field and asked him to take some bread and cheese to three of his brothers who were fighting on the battlefield. The Israelites had gone to war with the Philistines—a seafaring people who had moved to Palestine and settled along the coast. The Israelites were clustered in the mountains, still under the leadership of Saul. During the battle, the Philistines set up camp along the southern ridge of the Valley of Elah, and the Israelites pitched their tents on the north. With a valley between them, the two warring factions met in the middle each day to fight—or at least that's what was supposed to happen.

Every morning, as they met in the valley, the Philistines sent out their secret weapon: a nine-foot-tall giant of a man wearing one hundred pounds of armor. Goliath had a booming voice that hurled taunting threats at the Israelites all day long. Then on day forty, God said, "Enough."

David was still too young to go into battle, and I imagine he was pretty excited to get to see some real action. However, when he arrived, he didn't see his three big brothers and Saul's army courageously fighting the pesky Philistines. He saw them shaking in their sandals. He heard Goliath's threatening taunts and saw the Israelite warriors' weak-kneed retreat.

"Who is this uncircumcised Philistine that he should defy the armies of the living God?" David asked with indignation (1 Sam. 17:26). Then his eldest brother, Eliab, spoke up. Remember him? Older, taller, handsome firstborn? He was mad. Scripture says he "burned with anger" (v. 28). I suspect he had been burning with anger for about four years—ever since Samuel had passed over him and anointed his kid brother to be the next king.

"Why have you come down here?" Eliab said. "And with whom did you leave those few sheep in the wilderness? I know how conceited you are and how wicked your heart is; you came down only to watch the battle" (v. 28).

Eliab questioned David's motives and his character. I don't know of anything more heartbreaking for me than to be questioned in those two areas. I tend to fall apart, but not David.

"'Now what have I done?' said David. 'Can't I even speak?'" (v. 29). Then he turned away to ask someone else the same question.

Oh, friend, when God chooses you, anoints you, and appoints you for a specific task of great magnitude, there will always be those who question you, criticize you, and try their best to belittle you. When you dare to live bold, there will be those who will question your motives, your methods, and your means to accomplish what God has called you to do. Someone once said, "If you want to avoid criticism, you just have to do nothing, say nothing, and be nothing." I'll never be that person. I know you won't either.

I love what David did in the face of criticism. He turned away.

You know what you need to do? When it comes to living bold, you need to learn to turn away from the doubters, the joy stealers, and the confidence crushers. When you start living bold and saying yes to God, you will be criticized. Some people just have the gift of discouragement. You need to learn to turn away from the naysayers and toward the God who says you can do all things through Christ who gives you strength (Phil. 4:13).

Notice who tried to discourage David—his brother. It may be a family member who tries to talk you out of living bold. It may be a brother or sister in Christ who tells you to calm down. It may be the devil who whispers in your ear that you can't, you aren't, you never will.

This is where many stop short of experiencing the abundant life, of tasting the salt of thriving faith on their tongues, of possessing the promises of God. When they are criticized, belittled, or maligned by someone whose opinion they think matters, they stop. Not David. And hopefully not you.

Remember, the devil is determined to do his best to discourage your calling, demean your character, and diminish your confidence. He questions you: "Why have you come down here?" He belittles you: "With whom did you leave those few sheep in the wilderness?" He accuses you: "I know how conceited you are." He causes you to doubt your motives: "You came down only to watch the battle."

The devil will always accuse those whom God has called to do great things. That's who he is; that's what he does. He tries to trip you up and slow you down by tempting you to doubt your calling, ability, and courage. Turn your back on the accuser and your ear toward the Advocate. Move forward and take the next step of faith. David did.

Go After It

Someone told King Saul about this bodacious kid asking questions on the battlefield. Saul sent for him.

When David walked into the room, Samuel saw a kid. A brave kid, but still a kid.

> David said to Saul, "Let no one lose heart on account of this Philistine; your servant will go and fight him."
>
> Saul replied, "You are not able to go out against this Philistine and fight him; you are only a young man, and he has been a warrior from his youth."
>
> But David said to Saul, "Your servant has been keeping his father's sheep. When a lion or a bear came and carried off a sheep from the flock, *I went after it*, struck it and rescued the sheep from its mouth. When it turned on me, I seized it by its hair, struck it and killed it. Your servant has killed both the lion and the bear; this uncircumcised Philistine will be like one of them, because he has defied the armies of the living God. The LORD who rescued me from the paw of the lion and the paw of the bear will rescue me from the hand of this Philistine."
>
> Saul said to David, "Go, and the LORD be with you." (1 Sam. 17:32–37)

David had absolute confidence, not that he could kill the giant but that God would kill the giant through him.

Did you catch what Saul thought of David? "You are not able." "You are only . . ." Perhaps you've heard similar words, or at least thought them. "You are not able to do anything significant for God." "You are only a stay-at-home mom." "You are only a high school graduate." "You are only a secretary." "You are only a teacher." "You are only a burger flipper." "You are only a housewife."

Oh no you're not! You are a child of God who has been equipped by God, empowered by the Holy Spirit, and enveloped in Jesus Christ. You are chosen and called, anointed and appointed to do work God has prepared in advance for you (Eph. 2:10). When the naysayers, the enemy, or even your own negative thinking begins to tell you otherwise, remind yourself of all the ways God has been faithful to you in the past. That's what David did. And he went after it.

David never said *he* could kill the giant. He said *God* would. And that is the attitude every one of us who decides to live bold must have. It is not that we are going to pull ourselves up by our own proverbial bootstraps and dream big dreams of our own making. No, we are going to become men and women who listen to God's directives, seize the opportunities He places before us, and trust that He will do His work for us and through us.

Take Action

Saul tried to dress David in his armor, but David refused. It was as if he said, "I can't be you. I have to be me." He knew he was fearfully and wonderfully made, and he couldn't be anybody other than who he was. It's an armor-heavy burden to try to be like someone else. You look at how someone else does mighty things for God and think, *I want to be like her.* But God doesn't intend for you to be like her. He made her to be her. And He's made you to be you.

My ministry partner, Gwen Smith, jumps around like Christopher Robin's Tigger on steroids. I'm just not that bouncy, but sometimes I want to be. Then God says to me, "Just be good at being you."

When God calls you to a task, you will never succeed if you simply try to do it like someone else. You need to be you. You *get* to be you. David needed to be David. And he did it well.

He understood his God-given ability, so he gathered five smooth stones from a stream and met the giant on the battlefield. He knew it isn't how big your giant is but how big your God is that matters. And David served a big God. So do you.

> David said to the Philistine, "You come against me with sword and spear and javelin, but I come against you in the name of the Lord Almighty, the God of the armies of Israel, whom you have defied. This day the Lord will deliver you into my hands, and I'll strike you down and cut off your head. This very day I will give the carcasses of the Philistine army to the birds and the wild animals, and the whole world will know that there is a God in Israel. All those gathered here will know that it is not by sword or spear that the Lord saves; for the battle is the Lord's, and he will give all of you into our hands."
>
> As the Philistine moved closer to attack him, David ran quickly toward the battle line to meet him. Reaching into his bag and taking out a stone, he slung it and struck the Philistine on the forehead. (1 Sam. 17:45–49)

Okay. Hit the pause button right here. If you struck someone in the forehead, which way would you predict that person would fall? I'm thinking you just answered, "Backward." So let's keep reading.

"The stone sank into his forehead, and he fell facedown on the ground" (v. 49).

I get so excited every time I read that line, "and he fell facedown on the ground." Not backward, but forward. Why did the giant fall facedown? Because David threw the stone, but God killed the giant—pushed him right over. And so it is with you and with me. As we move forward in faith, God will work for us; God will work through us.

185

Where had David learned his skills for attacking enemies? Where did he learn how to be such a good rock slinger? Out in the pasture, taking care of sheep. God was preparing him for what He had prepared for him. Don't miss that. God is preparing you.

It's interesting that David gathered five smooth stones because he really needed only one. And that's all you need. David recounted, "The LORD is my rock, my fortress and my deliverer; my God is my rock, in whom I take refuge, my shield and the horn of my salvation, my stronghold. . . . The LORD lives! Praise be to my Rock! Exalted be God my Savior!" (Ps. 18:2, 46).

What's Stopping You?

Since childhood, Allison had always wanted to go on a mission trip. She dreamed of traveling to faraway places, but fear talked her out of every opportunity that crossed her path. Finally, at age forty-five, she decided to move forward, though afraid, and travel to Tegucigalpa, Honduras. There she fell in love with the beautiful land and its people. She saw how surrendering to God's compassionate pursuit of these villagers and their humble circumstances reshaped and refaced the core of who she was.

Waiting for her flight home at the airport, Allison overheard another group of volunteers discussing a dental mission trip they had just completed. While eating one more *papusa* from a local Honduran fast-food booth, Allison asked their local contact, "Brother Darrell, have you ever considered starting a dental clinic?"

"Sister Goodman," he replied, "I would love to see that happen."

Suddenly, Allison knew this was more than a passing idea. It was a burning bush right in the middle of the airport, and God was calling her name. A flood of emotions ran through her. *Who am I to put a dental mission together? I'm a musician and a wife. I don't have the resources or the know-how. I don't know anything about dentistry.* What Allison *did* have was an urgency in her gut and a faith that God would supply exactly what she needed.

"It was one of those tangible feelings when you know that you know," she later told me. "I began to think about the fine dental care I'd received all my life and about the Hondurans who walked around with hurting teeth."

As soon as Allison said yes to God, He began filling her mind with ideas. Asking anyone for anything was out of her comfort zone, but it was out of her comfort zone that God was calling her to live bold. She wrote letters to some of her contacts and then waited for God to supply.

Two weeks before she was to return to Honduras to set up the dental clinic, Allison still had no supplies. "I was standing in my kitchen praying, singing, and confident that I had obeyed what God had called me to do. Now it was time to see Him provide. I must have said, 'Lord, who am I?' a dozen times that morning. I continued with my household chores and then the phone rang. It was someone from church asking if I had the soundtrack for the song 'Who Am I.' It was as if God winked at me and said, 'I know who you are, where you are, and what you need. I've got this; just rest.'"

Over the next week Allison was flooded with phone calls from local dentists. She received enough supplies to fill two seventy-pound crates with excellent dental supplies. In addition to the supplies, a man called and said he found something in his father's barn that might be useful. When Allison opened the two large cases, she discovered a portable military dental station that had never been used. A generator, air compressor, hand piece, and all the other gadgets necessary to provide dental care—brand spanking new. She was advised to insure it for $8,000 before traveling.

"As I was packing the cases and looking over the quality of the supplies," Allison explained, "God opened my eyes to see the greater picture of what had happened over the past two weeks. All I did was say yes to God and then follow through with the process. He knew exactly where the provisions were located. He simply asked me to trust Him, hold out my hands, and receive. If I had held on to my fear and refused to take hold of trust, those supplies would still be in someone's barn! God called me to believe Him for something bigger than myself—something impossible to accomplish unless He intervened. He wanted to teach me how to live courageously, step out faithfully, and believe boldly. And I did."

When David got up that fateful morning, he had no idea he would be conquering a giant that day. He was simply going about his daily routine. He was getting ready, even though he didn't know for what. Then when the opportunity presented itself, all nine feet of it, he was ready. And it very well may be that way for you, just like it was for Allison. You may be going about your daily routine when your Father presents an opportunity that, unbeknownst to you, He has been preparing you for all along.

Talk to that person in the checkout line.

Plan a mission trip to Uganda.

Adopt that child from the orphanage.

Start a Bible study in your neighborhood.

Volunteer at the pregnancy center.

Run for public office.

Give away 20 percent of your income.

Write a book.

Oswald Chambers wrote, "Readiness for God means that we are prepared to do the smallest thing or the largest thing—it makes no difference. . . . A ready person never has to get ready—he *is* ready. Think of the time we waste trying to get ready once God has called! The burning bush is a symbol of everything that surrounds the person who is ready, and it is on fire with the presence of God Himself."[3]

So what will you say when God taps you on the shoulder and says, "Now's the time"? Henry Ford once said, "Whether you believe you can do a thing or not, you are right."[4]

188

The other Israelite soldiers could have said the same words David said to that giant, and they would have been just as true. But they didn't. Because David had a greater awareness of who God is and a better perspective of what God does, he had the courage and confidence to move forward and live bold. I hope you do too.

eleven

Taking Hold of Your Promised Land

The good news is that Moses did finally lead the Israelites out of Egypt, across the Red Sea, and on toward the Promised Land. The bad news is that only two of the original two million or so actually crossed the Jordan and received the blessing God had promised. A trip that should have taken eleven days took forty years.

What could have gone so terribly wrong? If you asked the first generation of slaves set free, they'd probably blame it on their enemies: the Jebusites, Canaanites, Hittites, Moabites, or Amorites. But it was not the enemies that kept them out.

They might have blamed their slow progress on weak leadership, poor directions, or bad weather. But it wasn't the leadership, wrong turns, or the weather that kept them out. What blocked their entrance to the Promised Land was their ingratitude and their refusal to believe. And if we're not careful, those are the same two reasons we will miss out on experiencing the promises of God and the adventurous faith of life to the full. For just like the Israelites, we can be saved from slavery only to live the rest of our lives wandering in the wilderness of our own grumbling and unbelief—never taking hold of all that Jesus has taken hold of for us.

Think about all God had done for the Hebrew nation. He had brought them out of Egypt, freed them from slavery, parted the Red Sea, and then called the water back to drown the pursuing Egyptian army. He rained down manna from heaven, dropped quail from the sky, and poured water from a rock. Who wouldn't believe or thank God if he or she had witnessed all that? Who wouldn't live bold after witnessing such miraculous wonders? But history proves that men and women can witness God do mighty miracles and still not believe.

Yes, God led the children of Israel into the wilderness, but they were never meant to stay there—to die there. The same fate can happen to you and to me if we settle comfortably into the milquetoast, mediocre land of in-between rather than move courageously and expectantly into the land of milk and honey—life to the full, replete with precious promises and mighty miracles. And the choice is yours.

Are You In or Out?

Moses led the people under the blood-stained doorframes of the Passover, across the dry land of the Red Sea, and to the front door of the Promised Land. God guided them with a fire by night and a cloud by day. He took care of their needs and brought victory over every enemy they faced. And yet, when it came time to march into the Promised Land, the land that was theirs for the taking, they cowered in unbelief.

"Send some men to explore the land of Canaan, which I am giving to the Israelites," God instructed Moses (Num. 13:2). So Moses sent twelve spies to scout out the land. When they returned, ten gave the following report:

"We went into the land to which you sent us, and it does flow with milk and honey! Here is its fruit. But the people who live there are powerful, and the cities are fortified and very large. We even saw descendants of Anak there." . . .

Then Caleb silenced the people before Moses and said, "We should go up and take possession of the land, for we can certainly do it."

But the men who had gone up with him said, "We can't attack those people; they are stronger than we are." And they spread among the Israelites a bad report about the land they had explored. They said, "The land we explored devours those living in it. All the people we saw there are of great size. . . . We seemed like grasshoppers in our own eyes, and we looked the same to them." (Num. 13:27–28, 30–33)

The twelve spies were not sent into the land to assess the problematic obstacles. They were sent into the land to take a peek at the promised blessings and bring back a sampling of its richness. This was not meant to be an exploratory mission to case the joint. Their names were already on the title deed. It was supposed to be a trip to get the folks stoked about the promises that waited just beyond the wall.

Sending in the twelve spies was supposed to be the denouement of the story: the final part of the narrative when the strands of the plot are drawn together and the climax of a chain of events occurs. Instead, the story took a nosedive.

"But the people who live there . . ." Whenever we add a "but" to the promise, we're in trouble. And they were in trouble. Oswald Chambers notes:

Human frailty is another thing that gets between God's words of assurance and our own words and thoughts. When we realize how feeble we are in facing difficulties, the difficulties become giants, we become like grasshoppers, and God seems to be non-existent. But remember God's assurance to us: "I will never . . . forsake you." Have we learned to sing after hearing God's keynote? Are we continually filled with enough courage to say, "The Lord is my Helper," or are we yielding to fear?[1]

Guess who the people believed? They believed the ten spies who said, "We can't" rather than the two who said, "We can because God already has." They believed the wrong report.

All night the unbelieving Israelites cried and wanted to go back to Egypt, while Caleb and Joshua tried their best to convince them to move forward and live bold.

> The land we passed through and explored is exceedingly good. If the Lord is pleased with us, he will lead us into that land, a land flowing with milk and honey, and will give it to us. Only do not rebel against the Lord. And do not be afraid of the people of the land, because we will devour them. Their protection is gone, but the Lord is with us. Do not be afraid of them. (Num. 14:7–9)

No matter what Joshua and Caleb said, the people refused to believe. They had the opportunity to go into the land but not the faith to possess the promise. I cringe at those words, wondering how many times they have been true of me. I mourn the opportunities not taken because I lacked the faith to possess the promise. Evangelist Leonard Ravenhill said, "The opportunity of a lifetime must be seized within the lifetime of the opportunity."[2] And they missed the opportunity because of fear and unbelief.

Because they feared the battle, they lost the blessing. They clung to the cul-de-sac safety of the wilderness and preferred its riskless tedium to the adventurous boldness of believing God. The sin of unbelief sabotaged God's perfect plan—just like it can in your life, in my life.

Finally, God said, "Enough." "In this wilderness your bodies will fall—every one of you twenty years old or more who was counted in the census and who has grumbled against me" (Num. 14:29).

Instead of taking hold of what was already theirs, the Israelites wandered in the wilderness of unbelief for the rest of their lives. That entire generation died in their stiff-necked refusal to believe, except for Caleb and Joshua. They were one in a million. That's what I want to be. I'm thinking you do too.

So here's my question to you: Whose report are you going to believe? Are you going to believe God's Word is true—that you are who God says you are and God will do what He says He will do? Or are you going to believe the naysayers who say, "You can't," "You won't," "You never will"? Are you going to listen to the voice of fear that says, "I can't do it," or are you going to believe the voice of God that says, "I already have"?

A grasshopper? I think not.

Turn Grumbling into Gratitude

But it was more than unbelief that kept the Israelites from receiving the promises of God. Their grumbling, complaining, and ingratitude held God's best at bay. The Israelites had a big throw-down party after crossing the Red Sea on dry land. Miriam led the group in a celebratory dance, and they praised God with wild abandon. That lasted for about a minute. Three days, to be exact. After they had gone out into the desert, they stopped at a place called Marah, where the water was bitter. "So the people *grumbled* against Moses, saying, 'What are we to drink?'" (Exod. 15:24).

God instructed Moses to throw a piece of wood into the water. The water became pure and they drank. And they were happy, for about a minute. A few days later, they grew hungry, and they *grumbled*.

In the desert the whole community grumbled against Moses and Aaron. The Israelites said to them, "If only we had died by the LORD's hand in Egypt! There we sat around pots of meat and ate all the food we wanted, but you have brought us out into this desert to starve this entire assembly to death." (Exod. 16:2–3)

Then the LORD said to Moses, "I will rain down bread from heaven for you." . . . So Moses and Aaron said to all the Israelites, "In the evening you will know that it was the LORD who brought you out of Egypt, and in the morning you will see the glory of the LORD, because he has heard your *grumbling* against him. Who are we, that you should *grumble* against us?" . . .

Moses also said, "You will know that it was the LORD when he gives you meat to eat in the evening and all the bread you want in the morning, because he has heard your *grumbling* against him. Who are we? You are not *grumbling* against us, but against the LORD." (Exod. 16:4, 6–8)

So God gave them manna and quail, and they were content, for about a minute. Moving forward, they traveled to Rephidim and again grew thirsty. And again they—you know what's coming— *grumbled*.

But the people were thirsty for water there, and they *grumbled* against Moses. They said, "Why did you bring us up out of Egypt to make us and our children and livestock die of thirst?" (Exod. 17:3)

God commanded Moses to go ahead of the crowd, stop at Horeb, and strike a rock with his staff. When he did, water gushed forth and provided water for grumblers. And they were satisfied, for about a minute.

Sometime later, they grew tired of the manna and again complained about God's provision. Once again, they grumbled.

If only we had meat to eat! We remember the fish we ate in Egypt at no cost—also the cucumbers, melons, leeks, onions and garlic. But now we have lost our appetite; we never see anything but this manna! (Num. 11:4–6)

Oh, friend, we must beware of Egypt's seductions and deceptions. The truth is, the food of Egypt had cost the Israelites everything—their freedom and their children's lives. Egypt is more than a country in Africa. It is a state of mind that seduces sinners who have been set free to romanticize the past slavery and forget the shackles that had them bound. The seduction of Egypt has pulled many back to the bottle, back to illicit sex, back to a destructive relationship. The tendency is to remember the taste but forget the wretched rot in the stomach after the urge is indulged.

Webster's defines grumbling as "to complain in a persistent, bad-tempered way; to make a low growling sound."[3] The original word also applies to the sound an animal makes: "murmuring, snuffling, growling between your teeth."[4] "Grumblers," we read in the *New Yorker*, "need only a few small dissatisfactions to begin their grumble-some work; from there, one grumble leads naturally to the next. If complaining creates a crisis, grumbling creates an atmosphere."[5] Grumbling is an outward expression of an inward attitude of ingratitude. It squeezes eyes shut to God's goodness and keeps life small.

Gratitude is "a feeling of appreciation for a kindness or favor received."[6] The word *gratitude* comes from the word *grace*. Grace is getting what we don't deserve. Gratitude is being thankful for it.

If there is anything that will shut our eyes to seeing God's presence and working in our lives, it is ingratitude. It leaves us groping about in the dark for what will never satisfy the longings of the soul. The cure comes in capsules of praise, thanksgiving, and a grateful heart. Gratitude is the antibiotic of the soul to cure a variety of the world's ills and restore a sense of intimacy with God.

When you think about it, grumbling and complaining are a casual despising of God's sovereignty. We don't like how He's running things and we think we could do it better. Moses said to the people, "[God] has heard your grumbling against him. Who are we, that you should grumble against us?" (Exod. 16:7). In essence, the grumbling was against God, not against Moses.

Gratitude changes the lens through which you see your circumstances and frames them in the sovereignty of God. When we look at life through the lens of gratitude, God comes into view. We see Him. We hear Him. We detect His fingerprints on the darkest days and the brightest days. It disconnects discouragement from its power source and gives us the impetus to move forward.

Paul wrote to the Thessalonians, "Give thanks in all circumstances" (1 Thess. 5:18). We read that verse and think it rather nice. So we slap a sloppy coat of thanksgiving on life and go about our day. In reality, most people are thankful for very little.

Notice the Bible doesn't command us to feel thankful in all circumstances. Instead, it commands us to "give thanks in all circumstances." When I begin to praise God in a difficult situation, even if I don't feel like it, my perspective changes. That was a lesson Corrie ten Boom learned from her sister Betsie as they suffered together in a German concentration camp during World War II. They lived in Barracks 28 in overcrowded, filthy conditions and nauseating stench. Reeking straw. Rancid beds. Overflowing toilets. And fleas. Everywhere fleas.

On their first day in the barracks, as Corrie was fighting the nausea from the reeking straw, and the fleas were biting her one after another, she cried out, "Betsie, how can we live in such a place!" And Betsie remembered a Bible verse they had read that very day. First Thessalonians 5:18: "Give thanks in all circumstances."

"That's it, Corrie!" Betsie exclaimed. "That's His answer. 'Give thanks in all circumstances!' That's what we can do. We can start right now to thank God for every single thing about this new barracks!"

Corrie stared at her sister, then around the dark, foul-aired room, and wondered what in the world they had to be thankful for. With Betsie's help, she agreed to give thanks for the facts that they were together, that they had sneaked a Bible into the camp, and that the overcrowded conditions made it possible for more women to hear the Scriptures when they read each day. But she could not see clear to thank God for the fleas.

"The fleas!" she cried. "This is too much, Betsie. There's no way even God can make me grateful for a flea."

"'Give thanks in all circumstances,'" Betsie quoted. "It doesn't say, 'in pleasant circumstances.' Fleas are part of this place where God has put us."

And so they stood between tiers of bunks and gave thanks for fleas. But this time Corrie was sure Betsie was wrong.

One evening Corrie got back to the barracks late from a wood-gathering foray outside the walls. Betsie was waiting for her, as always, so they could go through the food line together. Her eyes were twinkling.

"You're looking extraordinarily pleased with yourself," Corrie told her.

"You know, we've never understood why we had so much freedom in the big room," Betsie replied. "Well—I've found out. This afternoon, there'd been confusion in our knitting group about sock sizes and they asked the supervisor to come and settle it. But she wouldn't. She wouldn't step through the door and neither would the guards. And you know why?"

Betsie could not keep the triumph from her voice. "Because of the fleas! That's what she said. That place is crawling with fleas!"[7]

Sometimes I don't see God in difficult situations, but I still can praise Him because I know He is there. Gratitude changes the lens through which we see the circumstances in our little slice of time. Thanksgiving changes our perspective despite shattered dreams, broken relationships, and heartrending circumstances. It changes our perspective in the accumulation of little nuisances in just plain old everyday life.

Gratitude is one of the most significant aspects of our relationship with God. Looking back on all the ways God has blessed you will steady your feet in shaky times, no matter what you're going through. As you praise God for who He is and thank Him for what He's done, your perspective of Him grows larger and your problems grow smaller.

Live Gratefully Contagious

Have you ever noticed just how contagious grumbling is? Someone complains, and the next thing you know you've joined in and are complaining right along with them.

How do you think grumbling started with the children of Israel in the wilderness? I think it went like this: One person picked up her manna for the day and said, "You know, I'm sick of this manna." Then someone else picked up his and said, "Come to think about it, I'm sick of it too." Then a neighbor agreed and it spread, and it spread, and it spread. Next thing you know two million people are grumbling and complaining. Then a sea of ingrates wandered around the desert for forty years.

But just as grumbling ingratitude is infectious, so is grateful gratitude. One day I was in the airport headed to New Jersey. It was a typical rush, rush, rush morning. Grab the bags, trudge through traffic, hunt for a parking space, follow the herd, wade through security, dash to the gate.

Folks aren't usually very friendly in airports. Eyes look straight ahead. Purposed feet slap the floor. Overstuffed bags roll behind. It's not that people are grumpy. They're just "flatish" (that's a new word for today).

On this particular morning, I looked just like everyone else. "Flatish."

Before settling in at my gate, I decided to make one last trip to the restroom. I'm so glad I did. It was one of the most joy-filled places I had been in a long time.

Gretchen, the "hostess" for this privy, had donned a silly little hat on her head with whimsical feathers waving about the top. If it wasn't for the official attendant's vest she was wearing, I might have thought she was on her way to Mardi Gras. With a spray bottle in one hand and a cloth in the other, Gretchen welcomed each "guest" into her "home." "Come right this way," she said cheerfully as she opened a stall door for her next visitor.

A woman in a green jacket exited a stall and Gretchen swooped in behind her. Squirt, squirt, squirt with the disinfectant. Wipe, wipe, wipe with her cloth.

"Right this way, madam," she said as she motioned to the next person in line. "This one is ready for you! Come right in!"

With all the poise of a valet opening the castle doors for a person of honor, Gretchen welcomed each woman as if she were the most important person in her day. I stood back and watched as this five-foot-five-inch bundle of joy wiped off toilet seats and cheerfully invited her next guest into one of the pristine stalls. Gretchen had an effervescent sense of joy—while wiping toilet seats. It seemed to come from a deep-seated heart of gratitude. And it spilled over to every single woman who left her station.

Women entered weary and worn and left with a skip in their step and a smile on their face. Some even lingered, as if they wanted to soak in just a little bit more before facing the world. I was one of them.

On the counter rested a tip jar filled to the brim with thanks. But I don't think the tips the women gave were for wiping the germs away from the toilet seats but for wiping the doldrums away from their hearts and frowns off their faces. And for some strange reason, I just wanted to give Gretchen a hug. I did. She didn't mind.

Gretchen reminded me just how contagious gratitude and joy can be, and how desperately I want to be a carrier.

Put Your Foot Down

Yes, the first generation of slaves set free was not allowed to enter the Promised Land. Their grumbling and unbelief kept life to the full at arm's length. But when the next generation came along, they believed God would do what He said He would do. They moved forward to take hold of the promises and lived bold to claim what their parents never saw. What made the difference? Let's take a look.

After the death of Moses, God said to Joshua, Moses's aide:

> Moses my servant is dead. Now then, you and all these people, get ready to cross the Jordan River into the land I am about to give to them—to the Israelites. I will give you every place where you set your foot, as I promised Moses." . . . No one will be able to stand against you all the days of your life. As I was with Moses, so I will be with you; I will never leave you nor forsake you. Be strong and courageous, because you will lead these people to inherit the land I swore to their ancestors to give them.
>
> Be strong and very courageous. Be careful to obey all the law my servant Moses gave you; do not turn from it to the right or to the left, that you may be successful wherever you go. (Josh. 1:2–3, 5–7)

It is that sentence, "I will give you every place where you set your foot," that stops me in my tracks every time. God had given the Israelites the land, but they still had to take it. They had to put their foot down. They had to take hold of the promise.

Just because God gives you a promise does not mean it is automatically yours. You have to believe it and take hold of it! Paul wrote, "I press on to take hold of that for which Christ Jesus took hold of me" (Phil. 3:12). In one sentence, that is what this entire book is really all about. To experience a thriving faith—the abundant life to the full—we must take hold of what Christ Jesus has taken hold of for us.

I just love miracles. Don't you? I love reading about times when God mysteriously and supernaturally intervened in someone's life, times when what was impossible with man became a reality with God. But almost every time God performed a miracle in the Bible, He required men and women to participate—to put their foot down.

Build an ark.

Lift your staff.

Fill your jug.

Gather jars.

Make a cake.

Blow a trumpet.

Give a shout.

Jesus echoed His Father's cadence in the New Testament.

Take up your pallet.

Cast your nets.

Stretch out your hand.

Wash off the mud.

Look in the fish's mouth.

Roll away the stone.

Stand up straight.

Cast your nets.

Go and tell.

Yes, God does miracles. And in every one of the above-mentioned marvels, God's power followed someone's obedience. The key to experiencing the abundant life of relationship with Christ is obedience, and most people don't even like the word. But it is the pathway to the faith you long for.

Oswald Chambers wrote, "Even the smallest bit of obedience opens heaven, and the deepest truths of God immediately become yours. Yet God will never reveal more truth about Himself to you, until you have obeyed what you know already."[8] If you haven't heard from God lately, perhaps He is waiting for you to do something He has already told you to do.

Don't Stop Too Soon

The battle plan to take the Promised Land was as simple as it was strange. March around the city of Jericho with all the armed men. Do this in silence once a day for six days. Then on the seventh day, walk around seven times with the priests blowing the trumpets. Have the whole army give a loud shout; then the wall of the city will collapse and the army will go straight in.

Now, that was a strange plan. God's infinite ways often don't make sense in our finite minds. Sometimes you have to be willing to look ridiculous and be radical to live a remarkable life. The choices you make when you feel God's nudge will become the hinges on which your destiny swings. Each individual decision you make, to obey or ignore God's promptings and directives, is a thread that weaves the tapestry of your life.

Jericho was tightly shut up. Sometimes it can feel that our promises are tightly shut up. That doesn't mean we give up. That means we suit up, step up, and keep moving forward.

God said, "See, I have delivered Jericho into your hands" (Josh. 6:2). Notice that verb tense. God did not say, "*I will* deliver Jericho into your hands." He said, "*I have* delivered Jericho into your hands." He had already done it, but they had to obey and put their foot down to receive it. I love how God speaks in past tense to our present problems.

But here's the conundrum: What do you do when what God says doesn't match up with what you see? When all you see is a big wall standing between your promise and your present situation?

There will be times when you are doing everything you know to do, and you still don't see any movement. The Israelites walked around Jericho for six days, and as far as they could tell, nothing happened. I'm sure it unnerved the people behind the wall, but as far as the walkers could tell, not one brick fell.

This is where many give up—when they don't see any progress. The son is still taking drugs. The daughter is still living with her boyfriend. The husband is still cold and aloof. The bank account is still hovering in double digits.

"God, throw me a bone," I cry. "Show me a little something! Let me see just a hint of progress! Can I see one brick fall?" And God says, "Keep walking . . . by faith."

Just because you don't *see* God working doesn't mean He isn't. Jesus said, "My Father is always at his work" (John 5:17). The writer of Hebrews notes, "So do not throw away your confidence; it will be richly rewarded. You need to persevere so that when you have done the will of God, you will receive what he has promised" (Heb. 10:35–36).

Today, you might be on lap number seven and not even know it. Joshua told them to march around Jericho, but he didn't tell them how many times they were going to have to do it. He just said, "March forward" and "Remain silent."

Suppose they had stopped on day six, each one thinking, *This is ridiculous. I'm not feelin' it. Not one stone has fallen to the ground. I don't see any progress. Those folks are probably in there laughing their heads off. I'm going home.*

They would have missed the blessing.

I wonder how many times I have missed the blessing because I stopped too soon. Perhaps you've wondered:

How much longer will I have to wait until God brings my prodigal home?

How much longer will I have to struggle with this unbelieving husband?

How much longer will I have to endure this dead-end job?

How much longer will I have to go without a job?

How many more laps will I have to walk around Jericho before the walls come tumbling down and I can take hold of my Promised Land?

I don't know the answer to the question of how much longer, but I do know this: tomorrow could be the final lap. Don't give up too soon.

Can I tell you something? Sometimes I get tired of writing books, posting devotions, and crafting blogs. But as I sit down to the keyboard, I realize that something I say might be just what someone needs to take that last lap around her walled-up promise. So I write. And then someone has the courage and sustenance to take one more lap.

Take the First Step

Living bold is full of uncertainty. God told Abraham, "Go . . . to the land I will show you" (Gen. 12:1). That's not a lot of information. Oftentimes God will not show you step two until you have taken step one. Again, if you haven't heard from Him lately, perhaps He's waiting for you to do something He's already told you to do.

Paul wrote to the Corinthian church, and to you and me, "'What no eye has seen, what no ear has heard, and what no human mind has conceived'—the things God has prepared for those who love him" (1 Cor. 2:9). Another translation says, "What eye has not seen and ear has not heard and has not entered into the heart of man, [all that] God has prepared (made and keeps ready) for those who love Him [who hold Him in affectionate reverence, promptly obeying Him and gratefully recognizing the benefits He has bestowed]" (AMPC).

Every one of those plans God has prepared, made, and keeps ready for us requires letting go of one thing and taking hold of another. It was this truth that gave me the courage and confidence to leave the land of in-between and venture into the plan God had prepared for me all along.

Isn't it interesting that Joshua told the men to walk around the wall in silence? I imagine it might have gone something like this:

"Look, people, the last bunch of Israelites opened their mouths with grumbling, complaining, murmuring, and *unbelief-ing*. That's not going to happen this time. Just keep your mouths closed. Don't say a word. Don't talk to the person beside you, in front of you, or behind you. You can pray, but that's it. Keep your eyes straight ahead. Focus on the goal. On day seven you can break your silence, but only with praise. That's it. If you can't shout praises to God, then maintain your silence. But know this. I'm going to shout praise to God and watch Him work. Now let's go."

Sometimes (most times) we need to talk to God more about what He would have us do and talk to people less about what He's told us to do. I don't know about you, but if I talk about something I feel God is calling me to do long enough, I have a tendency to talk myself out of it. Not Joshua. He moved forward and experienced a faith teeming with miracles, chock-full of wonders, and pregnant with adventures. And it all began with one step of faith.

Be the Miracle

Just like picking up the scent of approaching rain on a summer day, I sensed God was about to do something amazing. With the anticipation of a child on the eve of her birthday, I suspected God had a special surprise for me in a little country sandwiched between two continents—El Salvador.

My ministry partners, Gwen Smith and Mary Southerland, and I were headed to El Salvador with Compassion International. We knew of the gang violence, the impoverished children, and the lack of clean drinking water. We knew of the unsanitary living conditions, the stifling crime rate, and the loss of hope for many of its citizens. We also knew of Compassion International's work to break the cycle of poverty of its children, in Jesus's name. And now we were going to witness it firsthand.

Two years before, when I was speaking in South America, someone had given me a beautiful Spanish Bible with my name engraved on the blue leather cover. I don't speak Spanish, so it sat on my bookshelf unused.

Take the Bible, God seemed to say as I packed my small carry-on.

"But God," I argued, "that's an adult-sized Bible and we're going to be seeing little children."

Take the Bible, He nudged once again.

I packed the Bible.

We arrived in El Salvador late on a Monday night and joined our Compassion team. "Will we have the opportunity to sponsor any children while we are here?" I asked Justin, our trip coordinator.

"Yes," Justin replied. "I have five children who need sponsoring where we will be visiting."

He handed me five packets with pictures and descriptions of five El Salvadorian children who were living in poverty. A precious tiny girl dressed in pink. A cute little princess dressed in yellow. A pair of huggable preschool-aged boys. And then there was Miguel . . . a teenage boy who seemed out of place among this batch of elementary urchins.

"Is it more difficult for teenagers to find sponsors?" I asked Justin, never taking my eyes off this soul wrapped in teenage awkwardness.

"Yes," Justin said. "People usually want to sponsor the little ones."

This is your miracle, came the gentle whisper.

I clung to the packet and pressed it to my chest . . . letting his name roll off my tongue and into my heart . . . *Miguel.*

The next day someone brought a surprised and confused Miguel to the project I was visiting. He had had a sponsor in the past, but for some reason they had to discontinue their financial support. He wondered why he was at the center and sat with the translator to get his answer.

"How did you feel when you lost your sponsor?" the translator asked.

"I was very sad," Miguel explained.

"Did you pray for another sponsor?" she continued.

"Yes, I prayed. I prayed and asked God to help me. I didn't know if I would ever be able to come to the center and learn about God again."

"Miguel, God has answered your prayers," the translator said, beaming. "Not only has God answered your prayers, but your new sponsor is in the next room." (Most of the thousands of children who are sponsored through Compassion International never meet their sponsors.)

I stepped out to meet Miguel and explained that God had told me about him before I even came to El Salvador. I explained that while he was praying, God was answering. I told him God had seen him, that God knew him, that God was providing for him, that God loved him . . . and so did I. I took out the Bible with my name engraved on the front, wrote his name on the inside cover, and handed it to him.

He smiled and said I was his miracle.

With tears in my eyes I replied, "No, son, you are mine."

That's what happens when you decide to leave the mundane safety of cul-de-sac Christianity and venture out into the adventurous life of the thriving faith. That's what happens when you know the answer to the question, "Who am I?" When you allow the great

I AM to fill in your gaps. When you leave the past behind and reach forward to all that lies ahead. When you stop comparing yourself to others and revel in the uniqueness of you. When you believe God will work through you, for you, and in you.

You will experience a thriving faith filled with a wellspring of wonders and supernatural surprises. You will see miracles. And sometimes, dear friend, you will be the miracle.

Let go of all that hinders you or holds you hostage to a mediocre faith. Take hold of all that Jesus has taken hold of for you. Move forward with the promises of God blowing your sails. Live bold with Jesus at the helm.

Bible Study Guide

This Bible Study Guide is intended to take you deeper into God's Word to discover more about how to take hold of the faith you long for. You'll need a notebook or journal to record your answers. Each lesson is intended to be completed after reading the coinciding chapter of the book—lesson 1 with chapter 1, lesson 2 with chapter 2, and so on. Grab hold of your Bible, and even gather a few friends, and let's see how to take hold of that for which Christ Jesus took hold of you!

Lesson 1—No Turning Back

1. Read and record John 10:10. What is one reason Jesus came?
2. The Greek word for "life to the full" is *perissos* and means "over and above, extraordinary, more, greater, excessive, in full abundance."[1]
   - On a scale from 1 to 10, where would you rate your current experience of living life to the full?

3. Can you think of a time when your spiritual life was at its peak? Your excitement for Jesus at its best? Your feeling of nearness to God at its most intimate? Describe that time.

   • That time could be today! If so, praise God. If not, what were you doing differently at your peak times from what you are doing now?

4. What are some reasons you think Christians get stuck in a mediocre, lukewarm faith and stop maturing toward the adventurous, thriving faith?

5. What came to mind as you read about the trapeze artist's "letting go and taking hold" in chapter 1?

6. Elijah was one of the greatest prophets in the Old Testament. But there came a time when he passed the mantle to a younger man, Elisha. Read 1 Kings 19:19–21 and answer the following questions. (To get the backstory, begin reading in 19:1.)

   • What was Elisha doing when Elijah approached him? Was he in a time of prayer or simply going about his everyday life? How does this compare to where you are in life right now?

   • What did Elisha do to deserve this calling? What did you do to deserve yours? (See Eph. 2:8–9.)

   • What did Elisha do with his plow and his oxen?

   • What is significant about his actions?

   • What does this show about his commitment to let go of his former life and take hold of his new calling?

   • What does this tell you about Elisha's Plan B?

7. What did Jesus call Peter and Andrew to let go of? (See Matt. 4:18–20.)

   • Where do we find them after Jesus's death and resurrection? (See John 21:1–14.)

- How did Jesus reiterate God's call on Peter's life? (See John 21:15–19.)
- Have you let go of anything by God's directive but then gone back to it again? If so, what is God saying to you about that today?

8. What Elisha and Peter were doing at the time of God's calling on their lives weren't bad things. But sometimes God calls us to let go of a good thing so He can give us a better thing. Have you ever had that experience in your own life? If so, explain.

9. Is God calling you to burn the plow today? Is there anything in your life God is calling you to let go of? This isn't necessarily about leaving a job but about untethering your life from anything that hinders you from moving forward. It could be letting go of resentment, an unhealthy relationship, a shopping addiction, or a host of other situations.

10. What is one key lesson you can take hold of from chapter 1 for how to let go, move forward, and live bold?

11. Record and memorize our key verse for this study: Philippians 3:12.

Lesson 2—A Brand-New You

1. Look up and record the definition of *identity* from a dictionary.
2. Read and record 2 Corinthians 5:17. What happens to your identity when you become a Christian?
3. How you see yourself affects your actions and your emotions. How might the following thoughts affect a person's actions, reactions, and emotions?
   - *I can't do anything right.*
   - *I can do everything God calls me to do.*

- *I am a loser.*
- *I am more than a conqueror.*
- *I am an ugly, fat slob.*
- *I am a beautiful creation of God.*
- *I have to earn acceptance and approval of people and of God.*
- *I am fully accepted by God. He accepts me because of what Jesus has already done for me.*

4. A common saying among Christians is "I am a sinner saved by grace." But is that true?
   - When did you become a sinner? (See Rom. 5:12, 18.)
   - When did you become a saint or holy? (See Rom. 3:22; Heb. 10:10, 14.)

5. What do the following verses say about your identity before you came to Christ? Romans 6:17; 8:8; Ephesians 2:1–20; 5:8; Colossians 1:21; 1 Thessalonians 5:4.

6. What do the following verses say about your identity after you came to Christ? 1 Corinthians 1:30–31; Ephesians 2:11–20; 4:24; 2 Peter 1:3, 4.

7. In Paul's letters to the churches, how did he address Christians? (See Rom.1:7; Eph. 1:1; Phil. 1:1–2; Col. 1:2.)
   - Some Bible translations say "holy people" and some say "saints." The Greek word for both of these is *hagious,* and it means "holy one" or "set apart for holy use." It doesn't mean perfect.

8. How would seeing yourself as a saint who sometimes sins rather than a sinner who sometimes does right change the way you think about yourself and process information?

9. One reason Christians get discouraged is that what God says about their true identity doesn't match up with their behavior and emotions. Paul had that same problem. Read Romans 7

and summarize Paul's dilemma. What was the solution stated in Romans 7:24–25?

10. Making your mind, will, and emotions line up with your new identity is a process. That process is called *sanctification*. What is one important step in the process according to Romans 12:2?

11. You cannot act differently than you think, but head knowledge is not enough. What directive do the following verses have in common? Luke 6:46–49; Philippians 4:9; James 1:22–25.

12. Go to www.sharonjaynes.com/my-new-identity-in-christ and read the list of truths about who you are. You may want to print it out. Choose five of those verses that mean the most to you and explain why.

13. What is one key lesson you can take hold of from chapter 2 about how to let go, move forward, and live bold?

14. Review our theme verse for this study: Philippians 3:12.

Lesson 3—Don't Settle for Less

1. What do you learn about God's promises in the following verses?
   - Genesis 28:15; Numbers 23:19; Joshua 21:45; Psalm 145:13.

2. In chapter 3, we looked at the importance of believing God's promises are true for you. In the Greek, the original language of the New Testament, the word *pistis* is translated "assurance, belief, believe, and faith."
   - Record the definition of *faith* according to Hebrews 11:1.
   - The word *conviction* or assurance of things hoped for is the word *hypostasis* in Greek and means "reality, confidence, conviction."[2]

- What do you learn from this translation of Hebrews 11:1? "Now faith is the assurance (the confirmation, the title deed) of the things [we] hope for, being the proof of things [we] do not see and the conviction of their reality [faith perceiving as real fact what is not revealed to the senses]" (AMPC).
- Look up the definition of the term *title deed* and describe what it means.
- What does "title deed" mean in regard to you and God's promises?

3. To what does Ephesians 1:11–23 compare the power you have when you believe God?
   - "Believe" in Ephesians 1:19 is a present active participle verb. That means to believe is a continual action and could be translated "continually believe." How is this different from the verb tense in Ephesians 1:13?
   - How could a person who has believed or made a decision for Christ get stuck in Ephesians 1:13 and miss the thriving faith of Ephesians 1:19?

4. When I was eight years old, I spent a week with my favorite aunt. Aunt Bessie took me to a giant toy store and told me I could get anything I wanted. I looked at everything from a pink sparkly bicycle to Malibu Barbie. But in the end, I settled on a Mousetrap game. The truth is, I didn't think she really meant "anything" when she said "anything." So I settled for something I thought would be reasonable. Have you ever "settled" in your prayer life? Asked little, received little?
   - How are the following verses an invitation from Jesus to raise your expectations in prayer? Matthew 7:7–11; 18:19; 21:21–22.

- What does James 4:2–3 tell us about why we do not receive what we ask for? What would be an example of a "wrong motive"? What would be an example of a "right motive"?

5. Sometimes I ask people, "How can I pray for you today?" Many times I get the response, "Oh, I'm good. Everything's fine." A woman in the Bible gave that same response when a prophet wanted to bless her. Read 2 Kings 4:8–17 and answer the following questions:

   - Why did Elisha want to bless the Shunammite woman?
   - Elijah looked beyond the "fine" and saw into her heart. Oh that we would do the same. Why do you think she didn't ask for a son?
   - What was her response to Elisha's promise in verse 16?
   - Have you ever had the same response as you've read the promises of God?
   - Have you ever lowered your expectations of God because you didn't want to be disappointed?
   - What was the outcome of Elisha's promise?

6. We're not quite ready to leave this story yet. God does fulfill His promises, but sometimes they are not as neat and tidy as we would like. His answers to our prayers are rarely without struggle and hardship along the way. Continue reading 2 Kings 4:18–37 and summarize what happened.

   - What was the Shunammite woman's response to Elisha in verse 28? Have you ever felt that way? If so, explain.
   - Perhaps your dreams need a bit of resuscitation today. Pray and ask God to breathe new life into hopes and dreams. Mouth to mouth, eyes to eyes, hands to hands.

7. What is one key lesson you can take hold of from chapter 3 about how to let go, move forward, and live bold?

8. End today by praying Ephesians 1:16–19.

Lesson 4—What's in a Name?

1. What do you consider your greatest strength?
   - What do you consider your greatest weakness?
2. Read 2 Corinthians 12:9–10 and note what God said about filling in Paul's gaps.
   - What did Paul say about his weaknesses?
   - Where did his strength come from?
   - What does 2 Chronicles 16:9 say about God's desire to strengthen His people in their particular weaknesses?
3. How does the Holy Spirit fill in our gaps when it comes to prayer? (See Rom. 8:26–27.)
4. God said the name YHWH or I AM would be the name by which He would be remembered from generation to generation. However, He has many other names in the Bible, and each one brings to light a different aspect of His character and His ways—who He is and what He does. Read the following verses and note what you learn about God. Note how each one of these aspects of God fills in one of your gaps. You might want to read the surrounding verses to keep the name in context. I'll give you the Hebrew name for God in each of these verses.
   - Genesis 1:1 (Elohim)
   - Genesis 16:13 (El Roi)
   - Genesis 17:1–2 (El Shaddai)
   - Genesis 21:33 (El Olam)
   - Genesis 22:14 (Yahweh Yireh)
   - Exodus 15:26 (Yahweh Rapha)
   - Leviticus 20:8 (Yahweh M'Kaddesh)
   - Psalm 18:1 (El Sali)
   - Psalm 23:1–4 (Yahweh Rohi)
   - Ezekiel 48:35 (Yahweh Shammah)

5. God is not all that concerned about what the world thinks about Him, but He *is* concerned about what *you* think about Him. Read Matthew 16:13–16. What two questions did Jesus ask Peter?

   • What was Jesus's response to Peter's final answer?

   • Friend, I believe with all my heart that this is true of you as well.

6. Let's look at one of the many examples of how God filled in the gaps for the Israelites. Read 2 Chronicles 20:1–30, then go through the following exercises and answer the following questions:

   • Describe the Israelites' dilemma.

   • List five to six key points of Jehoshaphat's prayer. (See vv. 6–12.)

   • List five to six key points of God's answer. (See vv. 13–17.)

   • How do each of those points apply to you in a current battle you are facing?

   • How did Jehoshaphat encourage the people? Read verse 20 and put your name in it.

   • Notice when the people started singing and praising God. Was it before or after the battle. (See vv. 21–22.)

   • When did God begin to set the ambushes? (See v. 22.) What do you glean from that?

   • How did God fill in Israel's gaps and fight for them that day?

   • I know this is a bloody example, and one you and I will never face. But we all face battles—some daily. What can you learn from Jehoshaphat's prayer and God's response that you can apply to the battles you face on a regular basis?

7. What is one key lesson you learned from chapter 4 about how to take hold, move forward, and live bold?

Lesson 5—Looking in the Face of Forgiveness

We are going to look at a lengthy passage today. You can skim the chapters to keep the featured verses in context. What we'll see is a beautiful portrait of forgiveness.

1. Read Genesis 25:19–23. What did God predict about Rebekah's two children?

   • What do we learn about the boys in verses 24–28?

   • Describe what happened in verses 29–34. "In ancient times the birthright included the inheritance rights of the firstborn."[3] What do you think Esau thought about Jacob's actions the day after he had sold his birthright?

2. Read Genesis 27 and describe how Jacob stole the blessing from Esau.

   • "The ancient world believed that blessings and curses had a kind of magical power to accomplish what they pronounced. But Isaac, as heir and steward of God's covenant blessings, acknowledged that he had solemnly transmitted that heritage to Jacob by way of a legally binding bequest."[4]

3. Jacob feared for his life. He ran away to stay with his uncle Laban and married his uncle's two daughters. After fourteen years, Jacob decided to return to his homeland. But there was one problem: Esau. Jacob felt terribly guilty and was afraid to approach the brother he had maligned.

   • We're going to skip a lot of the story, but I hope you'll go back and read it. Read Genesis 32:1–21 and describe Jacob's emotional state about seeing Esau.

   • How did Esau respond? (See Gen. 33:4.)

   • Read Genesis 33:1–11. Describe the reunion. Complete Jacob's sentence: "For to see your face is like seeing _____ _____."

- How is seeing unconditional forgiveness in someone's eyes like "seeing the face of God"?
- It has been said, "We are most like beasts when we kill, most like men when we judge, most like God when we forgive."

4. What do we learn about forgiveness in the following verses? Matthew 5:44–45; 6:12–15; 18:21–35; Ephesians 4:32; Colossians 3:13.

- (Note: Paul was in jail, being unjustly and hatefully accused, when he wrote the letters to the Ephesians and Colossians.)
- It is incongruous to accept consistent, constant forgiveness from God and withhold it from other people.

5. Do you need to forgive someone today? If so, consider praying the following prayer:

- Lord, I come to you today to let go of my bitterness, resentment, and anger toward _____. I forgive _____ for _____. I choose not to hold on to his or her offense against me, but to let it go and place the offender in Your hands. I forgive _____ as You have forgiven me. I pray You will heal my emotional wounds and remove all bitterness. In Jesus's name, amen.
- Now, friend, let it go.

6. What is one key lesson you can take hold of from chapter 5 about how to let go, move forward, and live bold?

Lesson 6—Are You a Ruth or an Orpah?

1. So far we've looked at several areas where we need to let go of one thing to take hold of another. In chapter 6, we looked at letting go of shame and taking hold of grace. And while this lesson isn't about letting go of shame, we are going to

look at two particular women to see how one hung on to her old life and one took hold of her new.

- We tend to read the Bible through the lens of the twenty-first century. But during biblical days, a woman's world was more like that of our third world sisters. A woman depended on her father, husband, or son for support. Without a male relative to take care of her, she was vulnerable and powerless.

- Read Ruth 1 and explain Naomi's, Ruth's, and Orpah's situations. What did all three have in common?

- Why did Orpah decide to return to Moab and not move forward to Bethlehem?

- What did Ruth give up by leaving Moab and going with Naomi?

- What was Ruth leaving behind? What was she taking hold of? (See v. 16.)

- The Moabites worshiped Chemosh, a god that demanded child sacrifice. By leaving, she was making a decision to leave her Moabite gods and take hold of Yahweh—Naomi's God.

2. Read Ruth 2. Whom did Ruth meet and what were the circumstances of that meeting?

- There had been many years of political tension between the Moabites and the Israelites. Mosaic Law banned Moabites from the assembly of Yahweh's people to the tenth generation. (See Deut. 23:3–6.) How was Ruth a gutsy risk taker to glean in an Israelite's field alone?

- Where do you detect God's fingerprints in Ruth 2? Particularly notice the words of verse 3. Was the choice of the field random on her part? On God's part?

3. Read Ruth 3. Give examples of how Ruth was trusting God and living bold.

4. Read Ruth 4. What was Ruth and Naomi's happy ending?
   - Who was in the lineage that followed her son Obed? (See Ruth 4:21–22 and Matt. 1:1.)

5. What would Ruth have missed if she had refused to let go of the Moabite gods and take hold of the one true God? What would she have missed if she had stayed in Moab?

6. What became of Orpah?
   - I'm thinking you said, "We don't know. Never heard from her again." And that is the point. Compare the two women and explain how living bold made all the difference.

7. Carolyn Custis James writes, "Ruth is a powerful reminder that the most important thing in all of life—the purpose for which we were all created—is to know the God who made us and to walk through life as his child, no matter what it costs us."[5] How do those words define what it means to live bold?

8. We have been focusing on taking hold of God's promises, but did you know God is taking hold of you? Read Isaiah 41:14 and note what you learn about God.
   - How do we see this played out in Ruth's life?
   - How have you seen this played out in your life?

9. What have you learned about living bold from the book of Ruth?

10. So here's the big question: Do you want to be a Ruth or an Orpah?

11. What is one key lesson you can take hold of from chapter 6 about how to let go, move forward, and live bold?

Lesson 7—Even If . . .

1. Look up and define the word *fear*.
   - My dictionary used these words: "a distressing emotion aroused by impending danger, evil, pain, etc., *whether the threat is real or imagined*."[6]
   - Do you think most of your fears are real or imagined? Explain.
   - What does 2 Corinthians 10:5 teach us about taking charge of what we *imagine*?
2. Read Daniel 3 and answer the following questions:
   - What was Shadrach, Meshach, and Abednego's crime?
   - Did they know the punishment for such a crime?
   - What was their response in verses 16–18?
   - Take note of the words in verse 18: "But even if . . ." What does this tell you about their faith and their fear?
   - Who did King Nebuchadnezzar see walking in the furnace with the three young men?
   - What was the king's response to their trust in God? Record verses 28–29.
3. Read and record 2 Timothy 1:6–7.
   - If God does not give you a spirit of fear, then where does it come from?
   - Why would the devil want you to live in fear? (See John 10:10.)
   - What is one way your fear could actually backfire on the devil's scheme to paralyze your faith? How can you turn that pitchfork around and stick it to him?
4. Read Mark 4:35–41 and describe the situation.
   - Where was Jesus during the storm?
   - What question did the disciples ask Jesus? Have you ever asked Jesus a similar question? "Jesus, don't you care if . . . ?" If so, when?

- What did Jesus ask them in verse 40?
- What did Jesus's actions prove to the disciples?
- What do Jesus's actions prove to you about the storms or fears in your life?
- When the storm started, the disciples were afraid of the wind and the waves. After the storm ceased, they had a different type of fear—a holy awe. Record verse 41.
- Once I was teaching this story to a group of four-year-olds. After describing the storm, I asked them if they would be afraid if they were in a little boat in a big storm like this. One little girl shrugged and said, "Not if Jesus was in the boat with me."
- Take some time and ponder her words. Is there any boat in life where Jesus is not in there with you?
- Read and record Romans 8:35–39.

5. Look up and record what the following verses teach you about fear: Deuteronomy 31:6; Joshua 1:9; Psalm 23:4; Isaiah 41:10, 13; 43:1.

6. Look up and record what the following verses instruct you to do with your fears: Psalm 34:4; 55:22; 56:3–4; Mark 5:36; 1 Peter 5:7.

7. What are your greatest fears?
   - How do these fears hold you hostage or hinder you from living the way God wants you to live?
   - Is there any area of your life where you are not obeying God because of fear?
   - Is there anything you are avoiding because of fear? A calling? A relationship? An opportunity?
   - Is there any area of your life where God is calling you to live bold by pushing through your fear and taking hold of faith?

8. What is one key lesson you can take hold of from chapter 7 about how to let go, move forward, and live bold?

9. Let the words of Psalm 51:10 be your closing prayer for today.

Lesson 8—Uniquely You for a Reason

1. What happened in Cain's heart when he compared himself to Abel? (See Gen. 4:3–5.)
   - What was God's response in Genesis 4:7?
   - The Hebrew word for "crouching" is the same as an ancient Babylonian word referring to an evil demon crouching at the door of a building.[7] How is comparison like sin crouching at the door of your heart?

2. What happened in Saul's heart when he compared himself to David? (See 1 Sam. 18:1–9.)
   - What was the result of Saul's jealousy? (See 1 Sam. 18:10–11; 19:9–10; 22:17–19.)
   - Saul pursued David for approximately eleven years. Think of all the wasted time Saul's jealously cost both of them. What was the end result for Saul? (See 1 Sam. 31:1–6.)
   - Have you wasted valuable time comparing yourself to someone else rather than being exactly who God made you to be?

3. In stark contrast to Saul's reaction to David, how did John the Baptist respond when his followers compared him to Jesus? (See John 3:22–30.)

4. If there were ever two people with differing gifts, they were Peter and John. If John was the "one Jesus loved," then Peter was the one Jesus corrected. But Jesus wanted them both on His ministry team because they both had something important to offer.

- List five characteristics of Peter you learn from the following references: Matthew 14:22–31; 16:13–19, 22–23; 26:51–52; John 20:1–9; 21:1–8.

- In the book of John, John referred to himself as "the one Jesus loved" and "the other disciple." He never mentions his name in the entire epistle. What does that tell you about him? List five characteristics of John you learn from the following references: John 19:26–27; 20:1–9; 21:1–8. (Note: James and John were the sons of Zebedee; see Matt. 4:21.)

- In summary, how were Peter and John different?

- Suppose all twelve disciples had been like Peter? What would that have looked like?

- Suppose all twelve disciples had been like John? What would that have looked like?

- Why do you think Jesus had these two very different personalities as key members of His leadership team?

- What does this teach you about how your uniqueness is important to God and to the church?

5. What was Jesus's response to Peter when he compared himself to John?

- Answer this in your own words. (See John 21:18–22.)

6. How did Peter and John work together after Jesus's ascension? (See Acts 2:37–41; 3:1–10; 4:1–13.)

7. Read 1 Corinthians 12:12–27. How is this a reminder to be the best *you* that you can be and not try to be the best *someone else* that you are not?

8. Consider Romans 12:6 from *The Message* paraphrase: "So since we find ourselves fashioned into all these excellently formed and marvelously functioning parts in Christ's body, let's just go ahead and be what we were made to be, without

enviously or pridefully comparing ourselves with each other, or trying to be something we aren't."

9. What is one key lesson you can take hold of from chapter 8 about how to let go, move forward, and live bold?

10. End today's lesson by praying the words of David in Psalm 139:13–16.

Lesson 9—Down but Not Out

1. Discouragement doesn't always come after a negative experience. Sometimes it comes after a great victory, or simply as a result of exhaustion. Let's look at what I call "The Elijah Syndrome." Read 1 Kings 18, focusing especially on verses 16–46.
   - Was that a good day or a bad day for Elijah?
   - List some of the highlights of what happened.

2. Read 1 Kings 19:1–5. What caused Elijah to run?
   - Does that seem almost silly to you?
   - Where did he go?
   - What did Elijah say in verse 4?
   - Have you ever felt that way?
   - Why do you think he was so discouraged after such a great victory?

3. Read 1 Kings 19:5–8 and 9–15. What was God's response to Elijah in each of these passages?
   - My favorite line in the story is when God says, "What are you doing here, Elijah?" So many times I've longed to hear from God, and when I got still enough to listen, I've heard the same, "What are you doing here? Get up and get going!" If you are feeling discouraged, perhaps God is saying the same to you.

4. In chapter 9, we looked at several examples of how to get up and get going in the face of discouragement. Let's look at a woman who did just that. Read Mark 5:21–34 and answer the following questions:

- How long had the woman experienced bleeding?

- For women of that time, she would have been considered ceremonially "unclean," and anyone she touched would also be unclean. That means she had most likely lost her family and physical contact within her community. What else had she lost?

- Sometimes we don't search for God until we've run out of options—and she had. She was ready to take a risk—to let go of fear and take hold of faith. What did she have to let go of to take the risk of touching Jesus's robe?

- What was the result of letting go of the cultural norms and restrictions and taking hold of Jesus?

- What do you learn from this woman about pressing on in the face of very discouraging circumstances?

- Is God calling you to reach for something today? If so, explain.

5. Read John 11:1–45 and answer the following questions:

- What was the situation with Lazarus?

- What does verse 5 say about how Jesus felt about Lazarus's sisters?

- What did Martha say to Jesus when He arrived? (See v. 21).

- What did Mary say to Jesus when He arrived? (See v. 32).

- How does this show their disappointment in Him? Have you ever felt that way? If so, when?

- Jesus told Mary and Martha to get up and get going. Where did they go and what happened when they got there?

- Martha and Mary were disappointed that Jesus had not come and healed their brother. However, because He waited, a greater miracle took place. Has there ever been a time in your life when you were disappointed or discouraged because things didn't work out the way you had hoped, only to discover later that God had a greater plan in mind? If so, describe that time.

- What lesson can we learn about our own disappointments from Jesus's delay and Lazarus's death and subsequent resurrection?

6. Paul told Timothy to guard his confidence. (See 2 Tim. 1:14.) You don't guard something unless it is susceptible to attack. How does discouragement attack confidence?

7. What is one way you can guard your confidence in the face of discouragement and disappointment that are sure to come?

8. What is one key lesson you can take hold of from chapter 9 about how to let go, move forward, and live bold?

Lesson 10—Bodacious Women

In chapter 10, we took a look at rock-slinging David, who grabbed hold of all God had for him and lived bold. In this lesson, we're going to look at three New Testament women who did the same. Before we study these amazing women, let me set the backdrop of how women were viewed and treated in Jesus's day.

Women were not allowed to talk to men in public—even their husbands. They were not allowed to testify in court because they were seen as unreliable witnesses. They were not allowed to mingle with or eat with men at social gatherings, sit under a rabbi's teaching, or be educated in the Torah. A Pharisee began each day with a prayer thanking God he was "not a Gentile, a woman, or a slave."[8]

Men divorced their wives on a whim and tossed them out like burnt toast. They were not even counted as people.

In Herod's temple, the women were relegated to a lower level separate from the men called the Court of Women. In the local synagogues, they stayed behind a partition, away from the men. They could listen but were not expected to learn. Women lived in the shadows of society, and they were to be rarely seen and seldom heard. Much like a slave, a girl was the property of her father and later the property of her husband. (To learn more about how Jesus came to change all that, see my book *How Jesus Broke the Rules to Set You Free: A Woman's Walk in Power and Purpose*.)

1. With that backdrop in mind, let's look at three women and see how Jesus called women to live bold. Read Luke 1:1–56 and answer the following questions:

    • What was Gabriel's salutation to Mary? (See vv. 28–30).

    • What did he tell her was going to happen? (See vv. 30–33, 35–37.)

    • What was her response? (See v. 38.)

    • What did Mary have to let go of to accomplish what God had called her to do?

    • What did Mary have to take hold of to accomplish what God had called her to do? (See also Luke 2:19)

    • How did Mary move forward to accomplish God's call on her life?

    • How did Mary live bold to fulfill her calling?

    • Can others say of you what Elizabeth said of Mary in verse 45?

    • What do you learn about living bold from the mother of Jesus?

2. Read Luke 10:38–42. This is probably a familiar story, but I want you to read it with fresh eyes. Go back and read

the introduction to today's lesson before answering the questions.

- What did Mary have to let go of to step across the cultural boundary, enter a room full of men, and sit at Rabbi Jesus's feet to learn?
- How was this a radical move for a woman in her day?
- Jesus welcomed Mary. What did she take hold of in that situation?
- How did she continue to live bold? (See Matt. 26:6–13; Mark 14:3–9; John 12:1–8.)
- What do you learn from Mary's boldness that you can apply to your life?
- By the way, I think Martha entered the classroom too. Look at her response to Jesus in John 11:23–27.

3. Let's look at one more bodacious woman. Read Luke 13:10–17.

- Where would this woman have been sitting?
- Where did she have to walk to get to where Jesus was teaching? How was this a bold move?
- What did she have to let go of to make that walk?
- What was the synagogue ruler's response to her bold move (not to mention Jesus's)?
- What did Jesus call her in verse 16? Jewish men were often referred to as "sons of Abraham." How do you think this made her feel to hear Jesus say those words about her? Do you think she took hold of that blessing?
- What do you think she did after she was healed? I think she did a little dance and then sat right down at His feet to learn!

4. What is one key lesson you can take hold of from chapter 10 about how to let go, move forward, and live bold?

5. End today's lesson by thanking God for all the ways Jesus broke the cultural rules to set women free to move forward and live bold. Thank God for the ways He has done the same for you.

Lesson 11—Put Your Foot Down

I hope by the time you get to this chapter, your foot is on the gas pedal and you've folded up that lounge chair. I hope you have "yes" on the tip of your tongue. But I want you to do more than start something. I want you to finish it . . . and then start again.

1. Read Joshua 1. List every directive God gave Joshua in verses 1–10.
   - How do those same words apply to you?
   - What was the Israelites' reply to Joshua's commands? (See vv. 16–18.)
2. Read Joshua 2. What did Rahab have to let go of? Take hold of? Move forward with? How did she live bold? What was her reward? (See Josh. 6:23–25; Matt. 1:5, 16.)
3. In Joshua 3, the fighting men broke camp and prepared for battle. The priest took the ark of the covenant and went before them to the Jordan River. When exactly did God part the waters for them to cross over on dry land? (See vv. 14–17.) What does this tell about the importance of obedience?
   - The river was at flood level! How is this the icing on the cake when it comes to what God can do in the life of an obedient servant?
   - What can God do even if the obstacles of your life are at flood level?
   - What can you take hold of when facing your obstacles, or stand on when you're in the middle of them?

4. What does Joshua 6:1 tell you about Jericho? The people were shut up on the inside because of what they had heard about what God had done for the Israelites on the outside.

- What did God tell Joshua in 6:2? What is the verb tense of "delivered"?

- And yet, what did the people have to do to take hold of the promise?

- Remember: Just because God gives you a promise doesn't mean you automatically possess the promise. You have to move from knowing the promise, to believing the promise, to acting on the promise by faithful obedience to make it yours.

- How does Romans 4:21 dovetail with Joshua 6:2?

- Joshua trusted in God's promise, power, and provision. That gave him the courage to move forward and live bold. How about you? Do you have that same assurance?

5. On about day six of marching around Jericho, I can see myself starting to doubt the logic of it all. I know this is a silly question, but you need to say it out loud, write it down in ink: What would have happened if the army got tired and frustrated and stopped marching on the sixth day?

- Look up and define the word perseverance.

- What do you learn about perseverance from Galatians 6:9?

6. Israel marched in and took hold of their Promised Land on day seven. And, friend, my prayer is that you will let go of all that hinders, take hold of all that Christ has taken hold of for you, move forward in faith when God calls your name, and live bold as never before. What is one key lesson you can take hold of from chapter 11 about how to let go, move forward, and live bold?

7. Take a few moments and make a list of how you are going to approach life differently as a result of this study.
8. I am so proud of you for finishing this Bible study. If you made it to the end, I know you are serious about living bold! The following is a poem I wrote just for you—with a little inspiration from Dr. Seuss.

Oh, the Places You'll Go!
by Sharon Jaynes

Congratulations!
Today is your day.
The adventure of faith
Is but a yes away.

You have smarts in your head.
You have Christ in your heart.
It's time to live bold.
Take a step and just start.

You are not on your own,
So there's no need to fear.
You are God's gal,
So listen, so hear.

You'll see opportunities
All sounding real good.
About some you'll say,
"I don't think I should."

Others will come
And tug at your heart.
When the Spirit says yes
Then it's time to just start.

You know who you are—
A dear child of God.
He said it, He meant it,
It's not a façade.

You know who He is,
The omnipotent One.
"I Am who I Am."
He said it! It's done!

"What ifs" not a problem.
Your past is just that.
You're moving forward,
So go grab your hat.

Don't worry about life
When you haven't a clue.
God's got it, He'll do it.
Show you just what to do.

Remember dear Moses,
Who worried and fretted.
He took along Aaron,
Which he later regretted.

And don't forget David
With his rock and his sling.
With faith like that boy
You can do anything.

Remember, don't grumble,
And don't you complain.
Be grateful! Be thankful!
When you can't even explain.

Oh, the places you'll go
When you know who you are.
When you trust in God,
Oh, you will go far.

So be your name Mary,
Abby, or Shea,
You're off to great places
When you do it God's way.

You will move mountains.
When you listen and pray.
So say yes to God.
And be on your way!

Acknowledgments

Writing a book is like putting together a giant jigsaw puzzle without the box top as a guide. Some people provide the corners, some the sides, and a host of others give hints about the marriage of shapes that fill in the places in between. A special thanks to:

Lysa TerKeurst, for a decade of growth and stretching at Proverbs 31 Ministries as you encouraged me to live bold when my knees were shaking and my voice was but a quaver.

Gwen Smith, for picking up Eeyore's tail and pinning it back on when it fell off . . . again. You have been such an example of moving forward and living bold. As my husband says, "A day without Gwen is a day without sunshine."

Mary Southerland, for giving me a good talking to on the days I wanted to quit. You have been such an inspiration to keep going when times get tough.

Pam Farrel, for being such a wonderful friend and encourager from a distance. Your joy and love for Jesus are so contagious.

Gail Cooper, for sharing her story and her heart—for going to the hard places to help others deal with theirs.

Bill Jensen, for his *agenting* expertise and hours upon hours listening to me on the phone. (Yes, I know *agenting* isn't a word, but it should be.) More than an agent, you are a dear friend.

Rebekah Guzman, for believing in me and in this project. Thank you for allowing me to encourage women to let go, move forward, and live bold.

Editors Jamie Chavez and Wendy Wetzel, for dotting my i's, crossing my t's, and making this book the best it could be.

My prayer team: Bonnie Schulte, Cissy Smith, Van Walton, Cynthia Price, Dawn Lee, Debby Millhouse, Gwen Smith, Jill Archer, Karen Shiels, Risa Tucker, Kathy Mendieta, Lee Anne Howard, Linda Butler, Linda Eppley, Mary Southerland, Pat Edmondson, Kim Abe, BJ Crouse. You women have been so faithful. Prayer is not preparation for the work; prayer is the work! You have held me up and pushed me forward on more days than I can count.

Steve, my husband, for being my chief cheerleader in life and love. What an incredible blessing God gave me when He gave me you.

God the Father, who equips me; God the Son, who envelops me; and God the Holy Spirit, who empowers me to let go, move forward, and live bold. I pray that the words of my mouth, the meditations of my heart, and the ink in my pen will honor You and help others to embrace the life You've prepared for them . . . all of it.

Notes

Chapter 2 Who Do You *Think* You Are?

1. Beth Moore, *Breaking Free: Discover the Victory of Total Surrender* (Nashville: LifeWay Press, 1991), 75.

2. For a more comprehensive list of verses showing your true identity in Christ, visit sharonjaynes.com/my-new-identity-in-christ/.

3. Seth Godin, "Belief," *Seth's Blog*, July 29, 2006, sethgodin.typepad.com /seths_blog/2006/07/belief.html (accessed July 23, 2015).

4. "Simon Peter—Reed to Rock," *Know Your Bible* (blog), December 4, 2011, insightstolife.blogspot.com/2011/12/simon-peter-reed-to-rock.html (accessed July 23, 2015).

5. Neil Anderson, *Victory over the Darkness* (Ventura, CA: Regal Books, 1990), 43.

6. William D. Mounce, *Mounce's Complete Expository Dictionary of Old and New Testament Words* (Grand Rapids: Zondervan, 2006), 382–83.

7. Beth Moore, *Believing God* (Nashville: LifeWay, 2001), 200.

8. *Pickles* used with the permission of Brian Crane, the Washington Post Writers Group and the Cartoonist Group. All rights reserved.

9. Adapted from Ron Lee Davis, *Mistreated* (Portland: Multnomah, 1989), 84–86.

Chapter 3 You've Got What It Takes

1. Mounce, *Mounce's Complete Expository Dictionary of Old and New Testament Words*, 386.

2. *The New Lexicon Webster's Dictionary of the English Language* (New York: Lexicon Publications, 1990), 599.

Chapter 4 The God Who Fills In Your Gaps

1. J. I. Packer, *Knowing God* (Downers Grove, IL: InterVarsity, 1973), 183.
2. Sharon Jaynes, Gwen Smith, and Mary Southerland, *Knowing God by Name* (Colorado Springs: Multnomah, 2013), 41–42.
3. Ibid., 42.
4. Sharon Jaynes, *"I'm Not Good Enough" and Other Lies Women Tell Themselves* (Eugene, OR: Harvest House, 2009).
5. I first heard the idea of God filling in your blanks in a sermon by Pastor Steven Furtick at Elevation Church, in Charlotte, North Carolina.

Chapter 5 The Freedom of Forgiveness

1. Spiros Zodhiates et al., eds., *The Complete Word Study Dictionary: New Testament* (Chattanooga: AMG Publishers, 1992), 229.
2. Philip Yancey, *What's So Amazing about Grace?* (Grand Rapids: Zondervan, 1997), 98–99.
3. Charles R. Swindoll, *Joseph: From Pit to Pinnacle Bible Study Guide* (Fullerton, CA: Insight for Living, 1982), i.
4. Corrie ten Boom, *Tramp for the Lord* (Grand Rapids: Revell, 1974), 82–86.
5. Brian Zahnd, *Unconditional?: The Call of Jesus to Radical Forgiveness* (Lake Mary, FL: Charisma House, 2010), 2, 12.
6. Kris Woll, *Nelson Mandela: South African President and Civil Rights Activist* (Minneapolis: Core Library, 2015), 30.
7. Zahnd, *Unconditional?*, 71.
8. Ibid., 41.
9. Henry T. Blackaby and Richard Blackaby, *Experiencing God Day-by-Day* (Nashville: Broadman & Holman, 1997), 193.
10. Malcolm Smith, *Forgiveness* (Tulsa: Pillar, 1992), 6–7.
11. C. S. Lewis, *The Weight of Glory* (New York: HarperCollins, 1949), 182.
12. Francine Rivers, *Leota's Garden* (Wheaton, IL: Tyndale, 1999), 15.
13. Donald B. Kraybill, Steven M. Nolt, and David L. Weaver-Zercher, *Amish Grace* (San Francisco: Jossey-Bass, 2007), 25. Note: This book used the pseudonym "Amy" for Marie Roberts; however, she now wishes to be referred to by her given name.
14. Ibid.
15. Ibid., 46.
16. Ibid., 48.

Chapter 6 When Your Rooster Crows

1. Lysa TerKeurst, *Unglued: Making Wise Choices in the Midst of Raw Emotions* (Grand Rapids: Zondervan, 2012), 33.
2. Steven Furtick, *Crash the Chatterbox* (Colorado Springs: Multnomah, 2014), 137.
3. Diane Dempsey Marr, PhD, *The Reluctant Traveler* (Colorado Springs: NavPress, 2002), 155.

4. Brennan Manning, *The Ragamuffin Gospel* (Portland: Multnomah, 1990), 26.

5. Carole Mayhall, *Lord, Teach Me Wisdom* (Colorado Springs: NavPress, 1979), 155.

6. David Seamands, *Healing for Damaged Emotions* (Wheaton, IL: Victor, 1981), 310–32.

Chapter 7 Give Fear the Boot

1. Oswald Chambers, *The Pilgrim's Song*, part VIII. First published in 1940 by Oswald Chambers Publications Association; the material is from talks Chambers gave in Yorkshire in 1915.

2. Dale Carnegie, *Dale Carnegie's Scrapbook: A Treasury of the Wisdom of the Ages*, ed. Dorothy Carnegie (New York: Simon and Schuster, 1959).

3. Mary Fairchild, "What Is a Talent?" About Religion, About.com, christianity .about.com/od/glossary/a/Talent.htm (accessed July 14, 2015).

4. Ibid.

5. *Shout to the Lord: Stories of God's Love and Power*, foreword by Darlene Zschech (Tulsa: Integrity Books), 8–9.

6. Casting Crowns, "Who Am I," written by Mark Hall, *Casting Crowns*, Reunion Records, 2003.

Chapter 8 The Measuring Stick Will Get You Stuck

1. Furtick, *Crash the Chatterbox*, 34.

2. Beth Moore, *The Beloved Disciple* (Nashville: LifeWay Press, 2002), 87.

3. Mark Buchanan, *Your God Is Too Safe* (Colorado Springs: Multnomah, 2001), 134–35.

Chapter 9 Get Up and Get Going

1. Ann Voskamp, *One Thousand Gifts* (Grand Rapids: Zondervan, 2011), 22.

2. Sharon Jaynes, *A Sudden Glory: God's Lavish Response to Your Ache for Something More* (Colorado Springs: Multnomah, 2012), 133–34.

Chapter 10 One Rock Is All You Need

1. "Dairy Queen Worker Gives Blind Man $20 after Theft," *CBS This Morning*, September 20, 2013, youtube.com/watch?v=xQwF3KtXxXA (accessed July 14, 2015).

2. Mark Memmott, "Praise Pours in for Dairy Queen Manager Who Helped a Blind Man," *The Two-Way: Breaking News*, NPR, September 20, 2013, www.npr .org/blogs/thetwo-way/2013/09/20/224417791/praise-pours-in-for-dairy-queen -manager-who-helped-blind-man (accessed July 14, 2015).

3. Oswald Chambers, *My Utmost for His Highest*, updated ed. (Grand Rapids: Discovery Books, 1992), April 18.

4. Published in a 1947 edition of *Reader's Digest*, as seen in Quote Investigator: Exploring the Origins of Quotations, http://quoteinvestigator.com/2015/02/03/ you-can/ (accessed July 23, 2015).

Chapter 11 Taking Hold of Your Promised Land

1. Oswald Chambers, *My Utmost for His Highest*, ed. James Reimann (Grand Rapids: Discovery House, 1992), June 5.

2. Leonard Ravenhill Quotes, www.leonard-ravenhill.com/quotes (accessed July 14, 2015).

3. *The New Lexicon Webster's Dictionary of the English Language* (New York: Lexicon Publications, 1990), 425.

4. Joshua Rothman, "A Few Notes on Grumbling," *New Yorker*, January 22, 2015, www.newyorker.com/culture/cultural-comment/notes-grumbling (accessed July 14, 2015).

5. Ibid.

6. *The New Lexicon Webster's Dictionary of the English Language*, 417.

7. Adapted from Corrie ten Boom, *The Hiding Place* (Old Tappan, NJ: Revell, 1971, 1974).

8. Chambers, *My Utmost for His Highest*, October 10.

Bible Study Guide

1. William D. Mounce and Robert H. Mounce, eds., *Greek and English Interlinear New Testament (NAS/NIV)* (Grand Rapids: Zondervan, 2008), 1139 (4356).

2. Ibid., 1186 (5712).

3. Kenneth Barker, ed., *NIV Study Bible*, 10th ann. ed. (Grand Rapids: Zondervan, 1995), 44.

4. Ibid., 47.

5. Carolyn Custis James, *The Gospel of Ruth* (Grand Rapids: Zondervan, 2008), 52.

6. *The New Lexicon Webster's Dictionary of the English Language*, s.v. "fear," emphasis added.

7. Barker, ed., *NIV Study Bible*, 12.

8. Aída Dina Besançon Spencer, *Beyond the Curse* (Nashville: Thomas Nelson, 1985), 56.

About the Author

Sharon Jaynes is an international conference speaker and best-selling author of twenty books, including *The Power of a Woman's Words*, *Praying for Your Husband from Head to Toe*, *How Jesus Broke the Rules to Set You Free: A Woman's Walk in Power and Purpose*, *Becoming a Woman Who Listens to God*, and *"I'm Not Good Enough" and Other Lies Women Tell Themselves*. Her books have been translated into several languages and impact women all around the world. Her passion is to encourage, equip, and empower women to walk in courage and confidence as they grasp their true identity as a child of God and a co-heir with Christ.

Sharon served as vice president and radio cohost for Proverbs 31 Ministries for ten years. She is the cofounder of Girlfriends in God, Inc., a conference and online ministry that seeks to cross generational, racial, and denominational boundaries to bring the body of Christ together as believers. Their online devotions reach over five hundred thousand subscribers daily. To learn more visit www.GirlfriendsinGod.com.

Sharon and her husband, Steve, live in North Carolina. They have one grown son, Steven.

One of her greatest joys is interacting with her readers. You can connect with Sharon through:

Email: Sharon@sharonjaynes.com

Facebook: www.facebook.com/sharonjaynes

Twitter: www.twitter.com/sharonjaynes

Pinterest: www.pinterest.com/sharonjaynes

Instagram: www.instagram/sharonejaynes

To learn more about Sharon's ministry and resources, inquire about Sharon speaking at your next event, or sign up for her blog, visit www.sharonjaynes.com.

Sharon Jaynes

Equipping Women to Live Fully & Free

Equipping Women to Live Fully and Free

SharonJaynes.com

Invite Sharon to speak at your next women's conference event

Join Sharon on her weekly blog or on
GirlfriendsinGod.com
for her daily devotions.

CONNECT WITH SHARON

 SharonJaynes
ThePrayingWivesClub

 @SharonEJaynes

 @SharonJaynes

 @SharonJaynes

give hope

Children sponsored through Compassion are known, loved, and protected.
Go to compassion.com/takehold and sponsor a child today.